High/Scope K–3

Curriculum Series

Science

Related High/Scope K–3 Curriculum Materials

K–3 Curriculum Guides (now available):

Language & Literacy
Mathematics

K–3 Curriculum Videotapes:

Active Learning
Classroom Environment
Language & Literacy
Mathematics

Related Publications of the High/Scope Press:

Young Children & Computers
High/Scope Survey of Early Childhood Software—1991
A School Administrator's Guide to Early Childhood Programs

Available from
The High/Scope Press
600 North River Street, Ypsilanti, Michigan 48198
313/485-2000, FAX 313/485-0704

High/Scope K–3 Curriculum Series

Science

Field Test Edition

by

Frank F. Blackwell
and
Charles Hohmann

Contributing Editor: Nancy Altman Brickman

The High/Scope Press
Ypsilanti, Michigan

Published by
The High/Scope® Press
A division of the
High/Scope Educational Research Foundation
600 North River Street
Ypsilanti, Michigan 48198
313/485-2000, FAX 313/485-0704

Library of Congress Catalog-in-Publication Data Number: 90-22885

ISBN 0-929816-25-0

Printed in the United States of America

10 9 8 7 6 5 4 3 2 1

Contents

Part 1: A Framework for K–3 Science

▼

Part 1

A Framework for K–3 Science

1

Basic Science Processes in a Developmental Approach

What is science? Science has been defined in many ways, but most definitions include some reference to the **active search for knowledge or truth**. In simple terms, science is the asking of questions—what? where? when? how? why? how much? how many?—about the organisms, objects, and systems in the world around us. And though scientists have conducted this search for answers in a variety of ways, most scientific advances have come about through a general pattern of working and thinking commonly called the **scientific method**.

The stages in the scientific method are familiar to most of us. The cycle starts with the awareness of a problem and a desire to solve it. Next come analysis of the problem, gathering of evidence through observation, development of a tentative solution (hypothesis), testing of the hypothesis through further observation (if it fails the test, starting again; if it is found correct, retesting it), and finally, stating a conclusion that provides a satisfactory explanation of the original problem. When used by professional researchers, this can be a refined, intricate, and highly technical process, but elementary-level children can also use elements of the scientific method in simple and straightforward activities. Whatever the level, an

Using Observed Facts: The Link With Reality

Observation links scientific thinking with reality. As basic as this principle might seem, even the Greek philosopher Aristotle failed to apply it. He insisted, on the basis of his own logical analysis, that heavy objects would fall faster than light ones. So widely was Aristotle respected that it was not until 1604—more than 1500 years later—that Galileo put the idea to the test by dropping a cannonball and a pebble from the leaning tower of Pisa. He observed that the objects fell at the same rate!

activity has scientific validity when two key elements are present: a desire **to solve a problem or answer a question** and a determination **to use only the observed facts** to seek the answer or solution.

Getting Started in Science

How can educators help young children get started in science? Let's look at some of the basic processes of science that are natural activities for young children and that provide a beginning for formal scientific exploration.

Good science starts with the process of **observation,** the most critical science capacity educators working with young children can foster. Effective observation is not just looking, but **looking with a purpose**, closely and systematically. Young children are good observers by nature; much of what they learn, long before they start school, results from keen observation. The child's capacity for keen observation has a biological base—the skills needed to sense danger, discover food, and perceive the trail home are vital to the survival of all creatures. In today's comfortable, safe environments, most young children do not need their observational skills for day-to-day survival; yet their curiosity and drive to learn from firsthand impressions is still strong. For children of this age, observation means using all the senses to explore—seeing, hearing, smelling, and tasting—and actively handling and manipulating materials.

In science education, we build on the young child's natural inclination to learn through sensory exploration and physical manipulation of objects. Adults help children develop their powers of observation by encouraging them to look more purposefully—to observe events over time, to count or document their observations, to take things apart to observe them more closely, or to plan observations to answer specific questions.

Another way adults encourage closer observation is by assisting children in using instruments to make their senses more acute. What we can learn from observation is limited by the acuity of our biological senses. Our eyes cannot see in the dark; nor can they discern objects that are far away or very small. We can hear many sounds, but in a limited range of frequencies. Smell, taste, and touch also have their limits. One aim of science has been an ef-

Observing: Looking With a Purpose

Children are natural observers. Here are some ways teachers can encourage children to make "just looking" into a purposeful, scientific activity:

- **Observing events over time:** "Let's take a picture of this tree every Monday and see how it changes from week to week."
- **Counting or documenting observations**: "How many insects do you see on the tabletop?"
- **Taking things apart to observe them more closely:** "Why don't you try untwisting that piece of yarn to see how it's made?"
- **Planning an observation to answer a specific question**: "I wonder if that ant can make it across the sidewalk without dropping that other ant."

fort to extend the range and sensitivity of human senses through the use of instruments. These instruments can range from magnifying glasses to a variety of precise measuring tools. The most important instrument of all, however, is the human brain, which organizes and interprets the observations collected. This implies another vital role for science educators: encouraging children to make sense of their observations by **using their developing thinking skills**—to classify, notice patterns, and infer causes, and to predict future events, based on the patterns observed and the causes inferred. These processes of thinking through gathered observations are what make the scientist.

Another basic science process—and another inborn scientific capacity that educators can foster in children—is **solving problems by a trial-and-error approach**. The young child is inclined to work at problems intuitively: When a possible solution occurs to him or her, the child tests it immediately; if that doesn't work, the child tries something else, and so on. Unlike the mature researcher, the child makes no systematic attempt to lay out all possible solutions to a problem and test them in an organized way. Though the child's method of just trying things until something "works" may seem unscientific, it can be a useful way to learn about the world. In fact, many important scientific discoveries have resulted from trial-and-error exploration, which can yield valuable insights about what works and what doesn't, what is relevant and what isn't, what is known and what is unknown. For young children, what matters is not the seemingly random way they test their ideas, but how the information gained is recorded, thought about, discussed, and acted on.

A closely related science process is **guessing at solutions** to problems. Here again, a natural inclination of children can come into play in science education. While a child's guess may be incorrect ("I'll bet the sugar will dissolve more quickly in cold water"), effective teachers recognize that guesswork is a part of any scientific effort and encourage children to make increasingly thoughtful guesses. For the child as for the professional scientist, a hunch sometimes *does* point the way to the solution to a problem.

This brings us to another science process and a corresponding capacity that educators can foster in children: **capitalizing on chance discoveries**—what might be called **serendipity**. Many scientific advances have come about through chance observations and happenings.

Organizing and Interpreting Observations

When children use their developing **thinking skills** to make sense of their observations, they are using basic science processes. Here are some examples of children "thinking out loud" as they organize and interpret observations:

- **Classifying:** "I'm going to sort out all the rocks with wavy patterns; all the speckled black, white, and pink rocks; and all the ones with shell shapes on them.
- **Noticing patterns:** "The branches on the Christmas trees get shorter and shorter as they get closer to the top."
- **Inferring causes:** "The sled always seems to go further with two people on it than with one. Maybe it's because it's heavier."
- **Predicting:** "If we add more ice and wait a while, we'll have more pop."

Such lucky accidents depend on the problem solver's ability to notice something significant, even when not actually looking for it. The investigator realizes that the discovery she or he has just made could be the beginning of some new and important effort. Lucky discoveries can happen in the classroom—if the teacher is ready for the unexpected and encourages children to recognize its importance. Following up on unexpected developments as they occur is good teaching as well as good science, because it gives priority to the child's unfolding interests.

Contrasting with the more spontaneous processes of trial-and-error learning, guesswork, and exploration of the unexpected event is another useful science process, **conducting planned experiments**. A planned experiment is what the term "science" connotes to most people, and though many major scientific discoveries have been made without systematic experiments, the controlled experiment is nevertheless the most powerful tool of modern science.

An experiment is nothing more than the process of causing something to occur under controlled conditions, closely observed. Experiments can range from a simple observation to intricate and carefully controlled procedures. The aim is to isolate the answer to the problem, first taking stock of what *is* known and then eliminating possible solutions. To find a satisfactory answer, the investigator must often study a large number of cases, with control groups at every fork in the path. Rarely can a result be considered final until it has been verified many times.

Of course, developmental limitations prevent most children in the early primary grades from conducting controlled experiments. Yet young children's experiments can still have validity. At this level, the crucial elements are a planned approach to a problem, a commitment to stay with the observed facts, and an openness to reinvestigation if new facts demand it. This process of planned experimentation fits smoothly within the High/Scope Curriculum, which emphasizes the process of planning, doing, and reviewing as a key element of the daily schedule in preschool and early elementary programs. The planned observation and reflective problem solving that occur in scientific activities can be seen as applications of the plan-do-review process (see Chapter 4).

Science—Both Spontaneous and Planned

Science discovery can be both spontaneous and planned. In the following three examples notice how trial and error, guesswork, lucky accidents, and planned observation all play a role in children's scientific explorations:

A Kitchen Experiment

Ivan, age 7½, loved to entertain himself by "making potions" in the kitchen. "I wonder how my orange juice will taste if I add some sugar," he said to himself, reaching for the sugar bowl. To his surprise the bowl contained sugar lumps instead of the free-flowing sugar he was used to. He dropped one lump, then two in the orange juice, tasted it, and pronounced it much improved.

"I wonder how plain water tastes with sugar," he said, dropping a lump in a glass of tap water. To his surprise, the lump sat on the bottom of the glass. "It's not getting dissolved," he said to his mother, who suggested that he try changing the water temperature. "I'll bet it will mix up faster in really cold water," he said, getting another glass and filling it with cold bottled water from the refrigerator. He dropped in the sugar lump and watched as it landed on the bottom of the glass. "It's hardly dissolving at all," he said. Meanwhile, Ivan noticed that the lump in the first glass of water had shrunk and crumbled slightly. "That one is slowly getting mixed up," he said. "I wonder what will happen with hot water."

Key Experiences in Science: Bringing a Focus to Science Learning

In this introductory section, we have tried to shed light on some of the basic processes in science, processes that are important for young children in the primary grades, just as they are for the mature researcher. We've explained that science starts with **careful observation** and the use of **logical thinking skills** to organize and interpret these observations. We've also discussed the ways that science is both a **spontaneous** and a **planned** activity, one that depends not only on careful measurement and planned experimentation but also on the readiness to learn from trial and error, from guesswork, and from serendipity. In addition, we've tried to show that these basic science processes are not foreign but in fact natural to young children; they are simply extensions of their inclination to learn about the world through direct observation and manipulation of materials.

As in all activities within the High/Scope Curriculum, **science learning is seen as an active process of doing and experiencing** rather than a passive one of absorbing information presented by the teacher. While the children engage in this active process, the teacher—using an awareness of basic science processes and of children's emerging abilities—brings focus to the child's efforts to answer questions and to solve problems. In doing this, the teacher uses six groups of **key experiences for science learning**. These key experiences describe scientific activity *as it is experienced by young children in kindergarten and the early primary grades*. They are intended to suggest the kinds of science experiences that we believe are appropriate for young children. For example, we don't train children to set up small-scale, but formal, experiments in which they state hypotheses, conduct trials, and interpret results. However, we do encourage them to explore, collect, and build, and, in the process, to observe systematically, gather data and materials, use systematic procedures to examine materials and data, notice trends and patterns, make predictions, and represent their findings. In this perspective, children's scientific exploration is not a miniature version of adult scientific method,

"Mom, will you help me—I want to do an experiment," he said, filling up a glass with hot tap water. "Let's do a test," he continued. "Exactly when I say Go, you start the kitchen timer and I'll drop a sugar lump in the hot water. We'll test how much of the sugar dissolves in 5 minutes and then we'll try it with some cold water." At the signal, his mother started the timer and Ivan dropped the sugar in the hot water. He watched as it immediately began to crumble, shrinking much more quickly than any of the other samples had. Satisfied that his question was answered, Ivan abandoned his project and began playing in another room.

After 2½ minutes, his mother called him back to look at his "experiment." Ivan glanced quickly at the glass of water. "It's all dissolved," he said.

"No it isn't," his mother countered, pointing to a small pile of crumbled sugar still visible at the bottom of the glass.

"Oh, yes, I can still see it," Ivan said, "but after 5 minutes it should be completely gone." He returned to his play in the other room.

Collecting on the Beach

A group of second- and third-graders were walking along a Lake Michigan beach, supervised by their teacher. The teacher had planned a collecting expedition focusing on types of rocks, and she expected that the children would choose rocks whose surface patterns, colors, and shapes they found interesting. There were a wide variety of attractive rocks on the beach, including pieces of though the undeveloped rudiments of mature scientific processes can be seen in children's efforts.

The six groups of key experiences are as follows:

■ **Observing: Looking with a purpose, collecting data**—This group of key experiences includes the activity most basic to the scientist; all other science activity is an elaboration on this basic theme of **looking with a purpose or a plan in mind.** When children observe, they are not passively recording their impressions as a camera or tape recorder does. Rather, their observing is a process of reconstruction and interpretation guided by their active minds—they literally see, hear, feel, smell, and taste what they are looking for. Of course, many stimuli do force themselves upon children's awareness—flashes of light, foul smells, sharp noises—and because of their survival instincts, they are biologically programmed to attend to these signals of potential threats. But there are enormous numbers of stimuli that can go completely unnoticed without children's active efforts to apprehend them. Because observation is such an active process, the capacity to observe develops as the thinking abilities of children mature and develop. The gradual changes in these capacities are reflected in the observation key experiences.

■ **Classifying and ordering materials according to their attributes and properties**—This group of key experiences describes children's use of logical thinking skills to organize observations into meaningful findings. The processes of classifying and ordering are fundamental to science. Organizing observations about plants and animals into a system of classification by kingdom, phylum, class, order, family, genus, and species was a crucial step in explaining the origins of similarities and differences among living things. Organizing data about the properties of chemical elements into the ordered system of the periodic table ultimately served as the basis for explaining concepts of atomic structure. When children notice attributes or structural patterns in living and nonliving materials and group or order materials accordingly, they are using this group of science experiences to develop a better understanding of the relationships among materials, organisms, and events in their environment.

■ **Measuring, tesing, and analyzing: assessing the properties and composition of materials**—In this group of key experiences, children use systematic procedures to make their senses more acute and their observations more precise. These related procedures enable children to

granite in many sizes and color mixtures.

After a while one of the children noticed a gray stone with a nearly perfect imprint of a fan-shaped leaf on it. Excitedly, she showed the fossil to the teacher and the other children. This sparked a lot of interest in hunting for "fossil rocks." The teacher picked up a few more fossils, less perfect than the first, and including many fossilized corals with repeated patterns. She showed those new kinds of fossils to the children. Soon most of the children were hunting for fossils. They quickly discovered that the patterns on the rocks were easier to see if the rocks were wet. This led some of the children to gather wet rocks at the edge of the water, while others developed a system of gathering a bucket of small rocks, wetting them, and then sitting down to sort through them.

Before long the children had amassed quite a collection of "fossil rocks," including imprints of leaves, small sea animals, shells, and coral. The children had also selected quite a few rocks that the teacher knew were not fossils but that children had identified as fossils because they had repeated patterns.

As the rocks began to dry out, the children were concerned that the patterns they noticed were fading; the teacher assured them that back in the classroom, they would explore some ways to glaze or polish the rocks, so they would remain shiny.

As the children were busy gathering rocks, a pair of children came upon another collector, who was looking for smoothed glass fragments. The children were fascinated by the smooth glass "pebbles" she showed quantify the properties and attributes of objects and materials, expressing similarities and differences in numeric terms and describing cause-and-effect relationships quantitatively. As they use these basic assessment techniques, children gain a deeper understanding not only of the materials they are examining but also of the importance of careful assessment.

■ **Observing, predicting, and controlling change: understanding causality**—While the previous groups of key experiences mainly involve ways of looking at materials closely and systematically, this group of key experiences focuses on **causes**. Here again, children are organizing and interpreting their observations, but the focus is on patterns and cycles of change rather than on attributes, properties, or structural patterns. As children notice and describe sequences of events in the world, they begin to notice regular patterns of change. This leads them to the heart of scientific inquiry, the effort to explain the causes behind the phenomena of nature.

■ **Designing, building, fabricating, and modifying structures or materials**—In this group of key experiences, children apply scientific knowledge as they solve "real-life" problems. As they work in this practical vein, children are developing their understanding of fundamental physical causes. The building projects that children undertake in this group of key experiences can range from simple to complex, and can include projects of the teacher's design as well as inventions that are completely child-initiated. As they work through the process of designing, testing, modifying, and improving a structure or material, children begin to learn the reasons for observed changes in the position, motion, shape, and size of objects and materials. They begin to understand how objects interact by pushing, pulling, holding, and bumping one another, and they begin to see how they can exert some control over these events by manipulating the factors involved.

■ **Reporting and interpreting data and results**—In this group of key experiences, children use language, pictures, and mathematical symbols to represent, and thus communicate, their observations and findings. Representation of observations and findings not only serves the practical function of **sharing results with others** but also helps children sharpen their observations and clarify their thinking.

them, as the concept of glass fragments that were not sharp or shiny was new to them. She also pointed out the colors of most of the fragments, most of which were either colorless, brown, or green. She said she had to look hardest for blue fragments, which were the rarest.

After this discussion with the collector, some of the children began looking for glass "pebbles," but they found only two smoothed fragments, of brown and green glass.

Back in the classroom, the teacher planned a number of follow-up activities to the collecting excursion. To build on the children's interest in glazing and polishing, she encouraged them to explore the glazing effects of several natural (water, egg white) and man-made (shellac, clear glue) materials on the rocks. She also brought in a tumbling rock polisher and several grades of sandpaper and encouraged children to try using these to polish the rocks. After the rocks were glazed or polished, she encouraged children to sort the rocks by their patterns. She showed them several references they could use to identify them.

Testing Sinkers and Floaters

A group of first-grade children were involved in a small-group activity exploring sinking and floating. At the teacher's suggestion, they were testing like-sized samples of various materials—tile, wood, particle board, cardboard, heavy paper, plastic foam, etc.—to see which materials were the best "floaters." They tested the materials by weighing them down with marbles, which they kept contained

Taken together with the content themes and activities given later in the book, these six groups of key experiences provide a process-oriented framework teachers can use to focus children's science learning. Keeping the key experiences in mind helps teachers recognize and build on the valuable scientific activity children engage in spontaneously as they explore the world.

In Chapter 2, we discuss the key experiences in more depth. First we explain the assumptions about child development that underlie the High/Scope Curriculum. Based on the milestones that occur in children's cognitive development during the K–3 years, we present a detailed breakdown of each group of key experiences. Next we present a thematic outline for K–3 science activities. Chapter 3 describes how teachers use the framework described in the first two chapters as they plan activities and work directly with children. Chapter 4 provides guidelines for classroom management: how to schedule and arrange the classroom for science activities and what kinds of materials to gather for science learning. Chapter 5 presents "case histories of effective teaching"—authentic examples of science teaching that embody the principles discussed in the previous chapters. In Part 2 of the book, we present a selection of science activities organized around three themes: Life and Environment; Structure and Form; and Energy and Change. Following Part 2 are two appendices: a child observation checklist on the science key experiences, and a detailed listing of useful materials for K–3 science activities.

by placing them on identical jar lids. The children were enjoying the activity and became very involved in a contest to see which "raft" would hold the most marbles before sinking. After a number of trials, a girl noticed that the cardboard samples became less buoyant as they got wetter (the cardboard had absorbed water). Though the teacher had been planning to suggest that children make a graph of the results of their tests, she decided to shift gears and encouraged the children to follow up on the girl's discovery. She helped the children devise a test of the effects of soaking the samples. Children tested samples of each material with marbles both before and after they held them under water for 1 minute. The plastic foam was found to lose no buoyancy from the soaking and was thus judged by the children to be a "wonder floater." ▪

2

A Developmental Approach to Science Learning

The High/Scope philosophy has two main features: a recognition of the Piagetian view of stages in development and a broad respect for developmental theory and research in general. Thus, in producing a science curriculum for children in kindergarten through grade three, we have attempted to use the insights of both Piagetian theory and the latest developmental research.

Our developmental perspective on science learning means that we emphasize *stages* not *ages*. We assume that within any one grade level, children will be at various stages and that some individual children will be at more than one stage in different aspects of science work. Although children progress through the stages in the same general sequence, the rate of progress varies from child to child. Some children will remain at the early stages longer than others will, and some may never achieve the later stages.

Besides the emphasis on developmental stages, another curriculum principle we have derived from Piagetian theory is our view that **children are active learners who construct their own understanding of the world** as they manipulate physical objects, explore with all their senses, and use language and other forms of representation to reflect on their actions. This view has led us to advocate an activity-based science curriculum that stresses active

Key Experiences for K–3 Science

The sidebars on the following pages present the six groups of science key experiences, each broken into three developmental levels. These key experiences form a major part of High/Scope's framework for teaching science.

learning experiences—for example, making collections; conducting surveys; building and modifying structures; and representing such experiences in pictures, graphs, and writing. In the High/Scope Curriculum, teachers are encouraged to plan a classroom environment that is rich in materials for children's hands-on activities. The classroom environment and teaching approach are designed to stimulate the exploring, discovering, comparing, combining, constructing, and representing that are the external reflections of the child's inward construction of knowledge.

This approach contrasts with more directive curricula in which textbooks, verbal explanations, teacher-led demonstrations, and short-answer worksheets predominate over direct experiences. Young children can and do learn from such secondhand presentations of knowledge. In fact, sometimes a verbal explanation or a demonstration may be the only effective way to introduce a concept or skill. Nevertheless, we view such activities as largely passive experiences that are not particularly engaging for children in the early elementary grades. Therefore, our approach to curriculum places a heavy emphasis on K–3 children solving problems as they work with and explore varied materials and pursue individual interests. Adults guide children in the exploration of scientific concepts by offering materials or suggesting tasks through which science concepts can reveal themselves. Children deepen their understanding of concepts, for example, when they explore friction-reducing materials for model car axles, when they sort a rock collection by hardness, or when they roll paper into tubes to strengthen a paper structure.

Stages in the Development of Children's Thinking

Of course, children's ability and inclination to solve such rudimentary science problems is both driven and limited by their developing cognitive skills. To offer appropriate and challenging materials and tasks, teachers of science must first assess their children's developmental status. Following is the developmental outline we use to guide our work with K–3 children.

Key Experiences in Observing

Level 1*—Preoperations: Intuitive Thinking*

- Using all the senses to investigate, explore, and observe the world
- Collecting materials of many kinds
- Observing color, shape, form, and pattern
- Initiating an observation to solve a problem or answer a question ("Let's watch and see if that ant makes it across the sidewalk without dropping that big crumb it's carrying.")

Level 2*—Early Concrete Operations*

- Looking at familiar things in a new way: observing closely, systematically, and objectively
- Taking something apart to observe it more closely (unraveling a piece of yarn to see how the fibers are twisted)
- Observing changes over time
- Observing the quantity of a material or the frequency of an event
- Using instruments (magnifiers, binoculars, slow-motion camera, tape recorder) to assist observations

From a Piagetian perspective, most K–3 children are passing through three consecutive developmental levels: **preoperations—intuitive thinking**, **early concrete operations**, and **late concrete operations**. The characteristics of children's thinking and learning at each of these levels are summarized briefly below. A fourth level, **formal operations—abstract thinking**, is presented to clarify the previous levels, with the understanding that most children will not reach this stage until their preteen or early teen years.

Level 1: Preoperations—Intuitive Thinking

The thought processes of young children at this level have been described by Piaget as "intuitive." This means that level-1 children draw conclusions or plan their actions on the basis of immediate physical impressions. Generally, children in the intuitive stage cannot imagine the consequences of an action unless they have tried it themselves or have seen it tried several times.

Intuitive thinking can be seen, for example, in the child who has two small pieces of wood that he wants to fasten together. Seeing a roll of tape, he reaches for it, takes a piece, and applies tape to the two pieces without any thought about the size or weight of the materials to be fastened or about the variety of other fasteners that may be available. The operative factors here are his past experiences in fastening things with tape and the ready availability of the tape. Had a hammer and nails been in plain view, he might have reached for them just as readily. This intuitive method of solving problems is often successful for the young child, but it has obvious limitations. As adults, we know that immediate physical impressions are sometimes misleading.

A classic example of the errors children make through intuitive thinking is their tendency to estimate quantities based on appearance alone. Seeing two equal groups of paper clips, one spread out on the table and the other piled closely together, young children in this stage typically conclude that there are more clips in the group that is spread out: They do not yet realize that the number of objects remains the same, regardless of how the objects are arranged, and that guesses based on appearances must be checked by one-to-one pairing of the two groups or by counting.

***Level 3**—Late Concrete Operations*

- Using audiovisual media for planned and systematic observations (photographing the same tree once a week for a year)
- Observing objects from different perspectives
- Observing the subsystems of an environment or structure to see how they interact ("We've noticed that the fish die if we don't add enough food, but too much makes the fish tank dirty.")

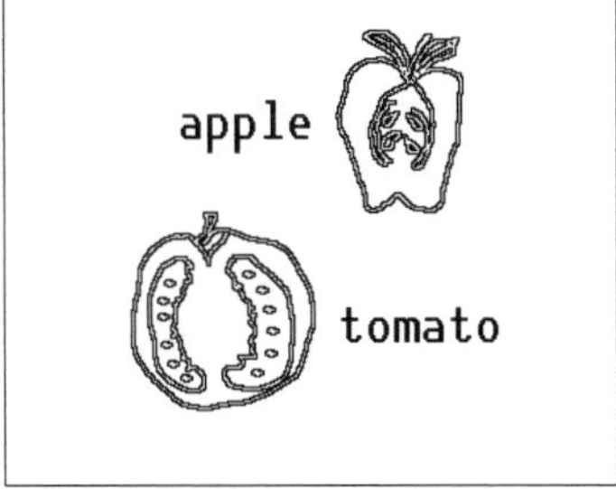

The observation key experiences encourage children to go beyond just looking to looking with a purpose, as in this activity (p. 116) in which children observe the seed patterns in familiar fruits and vegetables.

Returning to our example of the child taping two pieces of wood together, we can see some of the limitations in the child's intuitive way of solving his problem. He has not carefully considered any of the variables (the type of tape used, the weight and texture of the wood pieces) that will affect his success or failure. Though he succeeded in this instance in fastening the two pieces of wood together, with different pieces of wood, his unsystematic approach might have led to failure.

In spite of the limitations of intuitive thinking, however, it must be emphasized that children at this level **do have some rudimentary capacities to carry out basic science processes**. In addition to solving problems intuitively through manipulating physical objects, as in the foregoing example, these children are also beginning to develop the logical thinking and representational skills they need to organize and describe their perceptions. Children at this level can notice attributes, can classify in simple categories based on the presence or absence of one apparent attribute (such as "alive" and "not alive"), can measure in an intuitive way by making direct physical comparisons (for example, by standing back-to-back to compare heights), and can represent their discoveries in simple ways (by talking about what happened or drawing a rough picture of an experience).

Level 2: Early Concrete Operations

At this level, children begin to develop the ability to manipulate things mentally, as long as those things can also be manipulated physically at the same time. For example, a child can think abstractly about the problem of what makes the strongest block tower and may even consider a few of the variables involved—the size and number of blocks, for example. But as the child thinks through a problem like this, she is tied to the actual physical objects: she is constantly experimenting with them as she thinks about the problem. When asked to represent what she is doing, she is more inclined to demonstrate with the blocks themselves than to draw a picture or describe the problem in words.

Thus, concrete physical experiences are still of primary importance to the child in level 2. However, returning to the example of a child fastening two pieces of wood together, we see that the problem-solving abilities of the child have matured considerably since level 1. Unlike the younger child who reaches for the nearest fastener and ap-

Key Experiences in Classifying and Ordering Materials

Level 1*—Preoperations: Intuitive Thinking*

- Observing the attributes of objects
- Observing similarities and differences ("Both butterflies are spotted,") including differences on a single dimension (bluer, sweeter)
- Classifying materials into small groups based on common attributes

Level 2*—Early Concrete Operations*

- Observing multiple similarities and differences ("All the birds in this cage have feathers, wings, and pointed beaks but are many different colors.")
- Ordering objects according to variation along a single dimension (less rough, smooth, smoother)
- Observing similarities and differences in structural patterns and grouping objects accordingly ("This group of shells are shaped like fans.")
- Classifying materials into two groups based on the presence or absence of one attribute (dissolves in water/doesn't dissolve in water)

plies it to the wood, the child in level 2 approaches the problem more reflectively. Though she, too, may immediately reach for the tape, she experiments thoughtfully with it, making a series of modifications (such as trying out different lengths of tape, fastening the tape in different places) until she succeeds in fastening the two pieces of wood together. (If all modifications of taping fail, she may eventually decide to experiment with some other fastener, such as hammer and nails). This process of trial-and-error experimentation, in which the child tries out various modifications of a potential solution to a problem, shows the beginnings of mental analysis of a problem. But the analysis is still very simple, focusing on one possible solution at a time, with no concurrent sense of the large number of possible solutions.

The maturing of children's thoughts at the beginning of concrete operations is also reflected in their growing capacity for other basic science processes. They now can begin to observe systematically, looking for a particular change over time, for example; they are able to notice and describe multiple attributes and to classify objects by using more than one attribute at a time; and they can recognize and describe simple structural patterns. Measurement skills are also beginning to develop. At this level, children can learn to use measuring tools to measure in whole units, though they are not able to understand the part-whole relationships that are the conceptual basis for measuring in fractions of a unit.

***Level 3**—Late Concrete Operations*

- Observing symmetry and asymmetry in natural and manufactured objects
- Using an identification guide to look up organisms or nonliving materials (using books to identify trees or rocks)
- Classifying or ordering using two-dimensional matrices (ordering screws by length and diameter)
- Classifying hierarchically: grouping into categories and subcategories (birds, birds of prey, birds of prey that live in Michigan)

A sorting activity in which children classify shells they have collected by their shapes and surface patterns (p. 110) provides opportunities for the key experiences in classification and ordering.

Level 3: Late Concrete Operations

At this level, children's mental manipulations have grown more varied and complex. The maturation in children's understanding of part/whole relationships that typically occurs in this level is a developmental milestone that has broad implications for science processes. Children can now understand the relationship of the fractional part to the whole. Thus, a fuller understanding of measurement is possible, and the child can measure in subdivisions of standard units.

Also emerging at this level is the related capacity for hierarchical classification, in which the child groups materials into classes and subclasses according to increasingly detailed attributes. The appearance of this new capability has obvious implications for science activities. For example, this capacity allows children to understand the complex groupings and subgroupings of animal and plant species and to begin to see how one species relates to another.

Children's problem-solving abilities are also more mature than in level 2. Children can now mentally break a problem into its subproblems as a step towards finding a solution. For example, a child who is considering a wind-up toy that doesn't work has the ability to separate in his mind several processes that happen simultaneously. The child can understand that the car may not be working because one of its subsystems isn't working: Either the spring is broken and isn't catching; the gears don't mesh because they are jammed, broken, or bent; or the car has been sitting so long that the bearings are tight and need lubrication. This ability to mentally separate and then reintegrate several simultaneous causes is a feat that would be beyond the capabilities of the level-2 child. However, though the level-3 child is dealing with the problem at a more abstract level than would be possible for a less-mature child, he is still tied to concrete objects in his thinking. He is able to handle the separate issues of all the subsystems because they are easily observed and can be separately manipulated for testing as he is thinking about them.

Even in situations where all the interacting subsystems cannot be separated physically, the developing ability of level-3 children to sort out some of the multiple variables that can affect a situation increases the complexity of the problems they can work with. To illustrate, let's look again at the problem of a child fastening two pieces of wood together:

A child in level 3 would approach the wood fastening with more sophistication than a younger child, using her developing classification and ordering skills to sort out many of the relevant variables. For example, she could consider the advantages of the various fasteners that might be used for the job, classifying them into penetrating fasteners (screws and nails) and surface fasteners (tape and glue). She could consider screws and nails in a range of sizes, and she could order the various types of tape available (masking, cellophane, filament, electrical) by their stickiness and the strength of the backing material. She might also consider the properties of the materials to be fastened (weight, smoothness of surface, shape). Though the child at this stage could not set up a controlled experiment to separately analyze and test all these interacting factors, she can separate them mentally and consider them in a systematic enough way to make an ap-

Key Experiences in Measuring, Testing, and Analyzing

***Level 1**—Preoperations: Intuitive Thinking*

- Comparing the properties of materials ("This paper folds more easily.")
- Measuring by producing a length to match another length (cutting a string as long as one's foot)
- Counting events over time ("How many leaves will fall off this tree tonight?")

***Level 2**—Early Concrete Operations*

- Measuring properties and changes using standard or nonstandard whole units (weighing using the whole units on a scale; measuring elapsed time in sand timer cycles)
- Testing: assessing properties by comparing effects of standardized procedures (testing the strength of several fibers by tying them to a standard weight and observing which ones break)
- Analyzing: separating and measuring the parts of a mixture or material to describe its composition (separating and measuring the wheat flakes and raisins in a box of cereal)
- Using standard measuring tools (ruler, thermometer, calipers, scales, timers)
- Increasing or decreasing a causal factor and comparing the effects produced (comparing the effect on the color of water of adding a larger quantity of food coloring)

propriate choice of fastener. However, she is still tied to concrete objects in her evaluation of the situation: Her choice of the best fastener is dependent on her past experiences with fasteners and her present trial-and-error testing of the available materials.

Level 4: Formal Operations—Abstract Thinking

Level 4 entails the ability to deal with the abstract and hypothetical. Children at this level can think about abstractions; they are not tied to the concrete and the present. Most children in the kindergarten and early elementary years will not reach this stage; these mature abilities typically appear between ages 11 and 14 years, though some children may hover on the boundaries of level 4 in the early primary grades.

The ability to think in abstract, theoretical terms means that level-4 children can use the scientific method in its fullest sense. They can design a true experiment in which variables are controlled and in which all possible explanations for a phenomenon are systematically tested. Children at this level can also use mathematical and conceptual models to explore problems and generate hypotheses for scientific tests. To illustrate the problem solving of the child who has reached the level of formal operations, let's look again at a child who is fastening two objects together:

In contrast to the concrete-operational child, the child who has reached formal operations can explore problems of fasteners that are outside the realm of his direct experience, though he will use all of his past experiences in generating problems and hypotheses. Knowing from experience that bricks cannot ordinarily be fastened with nails or screws, for example, he might ask these hypothetical questions: Is there a penetrating fastener that could work with bricks? What would make it work? How could I get it into the brick? What would be strong enough to drive it into the brick without shattering it? He can now use concepts and models from science, engineering, and mathematics to develop reasonable hypotheses that address these questions and can design a series of controlled experiments to test them.

Complex problem solving of the kind just described relies on the maturation of a number of cognitive abilities and thus is beyond the capacities of most children in kin-

***Level 3**—Late Concrete Operations*

- Measuring using both whole units and fractions of a unit
- Estimating measurements ("It looks like it's about 2 feet tall.")
- Using a scale model to study the features of a larger or smaller object (model of a bicycle gear made from spools and rubber bands)
- Measuring the increase or decrease in a causal factor in order to relate it to the change in an effect("Let's see how much farther the car goes if we raise the height of the track 3 in.")

Encouraging children to build a yardstick balance and use it to weight familiar objects (p. 120) is an ideal context for key experiences in measurement. Children learn through this concrete experience that comparing is the basis for measurement. Depending on the children's interests and developmental levels, this activity could lead to many different key experiences.

dergarten through grade three. As developmentalists, we feel it is most valuable to encourage young children to apply those cognitive skills that *are* emerging in the K–3 years, rather than to drill them in using processes they can't possibly understand or to require them to memorize large numbers of science facts without opportunities for related hands-on work. To help teachers use our developmental approach as they plan science activities and interact with children, we present in the sidebars of this chapter a detailed sequence of science key experiences, an essential part of High/Scope's framework for science learning.

The Key Experiences: A Process-Oriented Focus for Science Learning

Given our basic assumption that learning is an active, constructive process, the all-important goal for teachers is to provide science experiences that encourage children to extend and modify their thinking about the world around them. In this view, learning the "right" answers is not as important for children as confronting new facts, observations, and experiences that call into question their ideas about the causes of common events and the structure and properties of materials. This process of discovery and questioning is internal and individual. Each child works from a different and personal view of reality that is shaped by his or her interests, previous experiences, and developing cognitive abilities. When learning is viewed from this perspective, the important goal is not that children reach particular learning objectives on schedule but that they continue to progress through the sequence of learning and discovery. Our approach, then, emphasizes the ***process* of learning** rather than the end result.

This notion of learning through discovery is innately appealing, and many teachers express support for it. The difficulty comes in applying it. When teaching focuses primarily on end results, learning objectives and sequences are relatively easy to specify, and progress is easily measured. But when the curriculum is process-oriented, there is a danger that classroom activities will lack focus and that teachers will lose track of children's progress.

Key Experiences in Observing, Predicting, and Controlling Change

***Level 1**—Preoperations: Intuitive Thinking*

- Observing and identifying a change ("The flower has closed up.")
- Manipulating physical objects to produce an effect or change (blowing out a candle)
- Repeating an activity that produces a change to gain awareness of possible causes (repeatedly pushing an empty bottle under water and watching as bubbles are released)
- Identifying a cause for a change ("The leaves are flying through the air. The wind must be blowing.")

***Level 2**—Early Concrete Operations*

- Observing and describing a pattern of change in events and movements (life cycles, cycles of motion, weather changes)
- Predicting a change in a situation from observation of change in other similar situations ("The sky is gray and the wind is blowing. I think it's going to rain.")
- Identifying more than one possible cause for a change ("The lawn mower won't start. Maybe it's out of gas or needs a tune-up. We have the most trouble on chilly days.")
- Testing an explanation for a change by acting to reverse it ("The plant is

To help teachers avoid these potential problems, we have formulated the **science key experiences**—a detailed developmental sequence of experiences that make up children's science activities. Teachers can use these key experiences as a process-oriented guide that will help them assess children's developmental levels, provide for appropriate activities, and recognize and encourage important science processes as they occur in the classroom.

As you read through the key experiences presented in the sidebars of this chapter, keep in mind the following: Each group of key experiences has been broken into developmental levels: level 1, preoperations—intuitive thinking; level 2, early concrete operations; and level 3, late concrete operations. In describing the experiences at these various levels, we have been guided by research findings on the development of cognitive abilities. It is important to note that the first five groups of key experiences primarily involve mathematical/logical reasoning and thus can be expected to develop at somewhat parallel rates in any individual child. However, the sixth group of key experiences, reporting and interpreting data and results, depends heavily on verbal abilities, which may or may not unfold at the same rate as the mathematical/logical abilities. Thus, a child who is at level 1 in observing, predicting, and controlling change, for example, may be at an earlier or later level of representational ability.

Of course, the key experience sequences we present are not meant to be absolute. For some children, the experiences described may occur in a different sequence; also, for some children, progress through one group of key experiences may be more rapid than progress through another group. Thus, this formulation of key experiences is intended as a resource that teachers can look to for *approximate* guidelines; it is not meant to prescribe or define a lock-step progression. For a child observation checklist that can be used to chart children's progress through the key experiences, see Appendix A.

How do the key experiences serve as a guide to teachers? Like traditional curriculum objectives, the key experiences guide teaching, but they are conceived very differently from most "teaching objectives." First, the key experiences are process-specific rather than content-specific; they are intended to be applied in many different content areas. Though they are listed here under particular levels, this is intended to roughly indicate when a particular learning capacity first appears in children; it is not meant to suggest that a defined goal must be accom-

wilting; let's try watering it and see if that helps.")

***Level 3**—Late Concrete Operations*

- Recognizing that a sequence of change (winding up a toy car to make it go) involves a sequence of causes and effects (Winding the key on the car activates motion in a series of gears, eventually resulting in the motion of the car.)
- Relating the magnitude of an effect to the magnitude of a cause ("A strong wind will cause many more leaves to fall off the tree than a gentle wind.")
- Beginning to recognize that explaining a change may require keeping some variables (possible causes) constant ("I think this toy car goes faster than the other one because it's built differently, but it might be because I oiled it before the race. Let's oil the other car, too, and then try racing them again.")

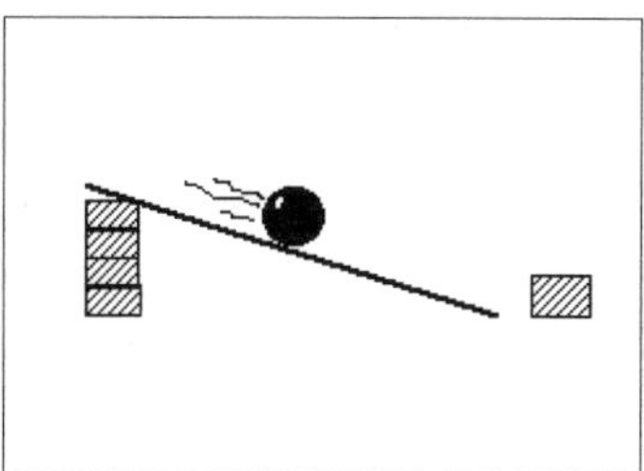

A simple activity in which children experiment with rolling various kinds of balls down a ramp to hit a target block (p. 170) provides a context for key experiences in observing, predicting, and controlling change.

plished at a particular point. It is assumed, instead, that all the capacities emerging at various levels will continue to be used later on in different and more sophisticated contexts.

Second, unlike traditional teaching objectives, which typically lead to structured exercises focusing, one at a time, on discrete skills or concepts, many of the key experiences coincide and interact in effective learning activities. Some types of activities clearly lend themselves to a particular group of key experiences (for example, a collecting excursion will usually lead to classifying and ordering). However, in the course of such projects, teachers will usually notice opportunities to foster the other key experiences. In almost any science activity, in fact, it may be appropriate, at particular times, to encourage children to observe closely, to measure, to describe cause-and-effect relationships, and to communicate or represent their findings. It should also be noted that observational experiences, the first group of key experiences, are inextricably linked with all the other science experiences. Clearly, a child cannot measure, test, analyze, classify, describe causes, design structures, or represent findings without also observing carefully.

Nevertheless, the fact that most learning activities are likely to involve a number of key experiences does not suggest that teachers should treat the various experiences as one. Instead, High/Scope teachers are ever alert to recognize the specific experiences children are encountering from moment to moment, so they can act to support them. Recognizing and taking advantage of these "teachable moments" is the key to effective teaching in the High/Scope Curriculum.

Learning the Key Experiences

Throughout this discussion of planning and teaching, we've continually referred to the key experiences as the all-important guide for identifying children's developmental levels and promoting developmentally appropriate science activities. To use our approach, teachers must **know the key experiences.** How do teachers familiarize themselves with this seemingly long and complex list? This task is not as daunting as it may appear.

It may help to remember, first, that the overall processes themselves—observing, classifying, measuring, testing, analyzing, noticing causes, predicting, building, and

Key Experiences in Designing, Building, Fabricating, and Modifying Structures or Materials

***Level 1**—Preoperations: Intuitive Thinking*

- Designing and building simple structures (making a garage for toy cars out of blocks and boards)
- Changing a structure to solve a problem in its design("Maybe the tower won't fall over if I use the flat blocks instead.")
- Comparing the performance of similar structures or materials ("The ramp works better this way.")
- Using plans supplied by others to make simple structures or materials (a paper teepee; flour paste)

***Level 2**—Early Concrete Operations*

- Designing and building more complex structures (realistic objects constructed with conventional building materials, tools, and fasteners)
- Building simple containers or environments for living things (an insect box; a windowbox garden)
- Improving a structure or material through trial-and-error modifications (varying the height and length of a ramp to increase the speed of a toy car; adding sugar or water to icing to change the consistency)

so forth—are straightforward and easy to recognize. In addition, many of the same processes are used as guideposts in other curriculum areas—measuring, for example, is an important process for both math and science. The "daunting" part is learning the specific developmental milestones in each group of experiences.

In working with teachers who are using the High/Scope approach, we have found that **familiarity with the key experiences grows from using them—not from memorizing the list**. If teachers consciously use the key experiences daily as a guide in planning and assessing science activities and in interacting with children, they gradually become comfortable and skilled in using them. Some teachers find that it helps to focus on one or two groups of key experiences for a day or week at a time, planning activities around those key experiences and looking for opportunities to foster them throughout classroom science activities. Such a focus should not be so rigid, however, that teachers miss out on opportunities to capitalize on other key experiences that arise spontaneously in the course of children's work.

Themes for K–3 Science

In addition to the key experiences, another major part of the framework for teaching science in the High/Scope Curriculum is a thematic outline. Traditionally, science content was thought of as a body of knowledge about certain physical phenomena and about the structure and form of living and nonliving materials. Physics—one "branch" of this body of knowledge—was defined as the study of heat, light, sound, electricity, magnetism, and related topics. Chemistry—another branch—was concerned with the analysis of substances and the description of chemical changes. Biology—still another branch—was primarily descriptive, concerning itself with the dissection, classification, and identification of living things.

However, by the mid-1950s and early 1960s this view of science was largely put aside. In keeping with the view of science as an active process of discovery, the tidy content boxes of the past were replaced with broad themes that cut across the old content "branches." Therefore, we have organized the activities in this book around three such "generic" themes: **Life and Environment**, **Structure and Form**, and **Energy and Change**. Within each theme,

- Using plans supplied by others to make more complex and functional structures or materials (making dog biscuits, making pinwheels)

Level 3*—Late Concrete Operations*

- Building structures with moving parts (latches, hinges, wheels, and axles)
- Building with simple electrical circuits
- Analyzing and solving problems in a structure by taking it apart, modifying parts, and rebuilding it (troubleshooting a problem in a wind-up car by separately examining the wheels and axles, the spring mechanism, and the gears)
- Identifying more than one factor affecting the operation or effectiveness of a structure or material (recognizing that the problem of fastening two materials together may be affected by the type of fastener—e.g., tape, screws, nails—the size of the fastener, the smoothness of the surfaces being joined, and the weight of the pieces to be joined)

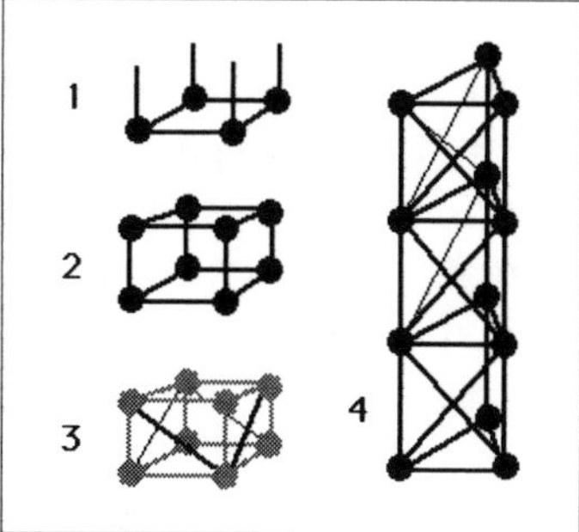

A science workshop in which children explore different ways to build lattice structures out of balsa wood sticks and miniature marshmallows (p. 138) provides an encounter with important key experiences in building and designing.

we include possible subthemes. This list of themes and subthemes is not intended to be exhaustive or definitive; rather, it is a working draft that can be modified by teachers to suit their circumstances:

- **Life and environment**
  Properties of living systems (growth, change, life cycles)
  Composition of living systems (derivative foods, fibers, other products)
  Management of living systems (habitats and environments)

- **Structure and form**
  Properties of materials (stability, function, interaction)
  Composition of materials
  Design and building of structural systems

- **Energy and change**
  Force (pushes, pulls)
  Energy transfers (physical change, motion)
  Machines

The broad themes we use are compatible with the approaches used by several currently available textbooks, which may be used as supporting materials by teachers working within the High/Scope approach. The specific topics and activities we include (in Part 2 of this book) under each thematic area are just a few of many possible topics and activities. Science leads can also be provided via almost any child-chosen investigative activity, and such leads will easily fit our thematic outline.

Together, the key experiences and the thematic outline we've just given provide a framework that guides teaching in the High/Scope Curriculum. In the next chapter, we'll provide specific strategies teachers can use to promote learning through the key experiences as they plan activities and work directly with children.

Key Experiences in Reporting and Interpreting Data and Results

Level 1*—Preoperations: Intuitive Thinking*

- Discussing observations
- Beginning to use scientific terms and comparative vocabulary in reporting observations
- Reporting sequences of events
- Reporting and representing observations using drawings, tape recordings, photos, or real objects mounted on charts

Level 2*—Early Concrete Operations*

- Recording and displaying numerical data
- Using models, drawings, and diagrams to illustrate oral or written reports
- Arranging collections and displays to present findings
- Using books, pictures, charts, and computers to gain further information

Level 3*—Late Concrete Operations*

- Defining technical terms in science reporting
- Using bar graphs, line graphs, and tables to present data
- Making models of objects and systems to show how they work (making a model of a stream bed, using sand and buckets of water)

3

▼

An Approach to Planning, Teaching, and Assessment

In the previous chapters, we have described the teaching framework for science in the High/Scope K–3 Curriculum, a framework that consists of the key experiences and a thematic outline. In this chapter, we discuss how teachers use this framework as they plan, conduct, and assess science activities. First we describe steps teachers can take to set the stage for science learning. Then, after describing several contexts for science activities, we outline some general teaching strategies that characterize the High/Scope approach.

Setting the Stage

Before teachers can plan specific science activities, it is important to **arrange a learning environment in which the discovery process can unfold.** This means selecting materials that are appealing to children and that lend themselves to the exploration of science facts and concepts. Chapter 4 will give detailed suggestions on gathering a range of suitable materials and arranging them in a classroom "science area."

Another important preliminary step is to **plan a daily schedule that allows for a variety of formats for science activities.** Ideally the schedule should include times for children to engage in relaxed exploration and unstructured observation; times for them to work on problem-solving tasks; times for them to work in large groups, in small groups, and as individuals; and times for them to work on short- as well as long-term projects. Obviously, not all these kinds of science activities can occur every day or even every week, but long-term planning should aim for such a range of formats. Varying the menu of activities in this way helps to balance teacher and child initiatives and offers opportunities for children to experience science concepts in different contexts. (For details on how to schedule science activities within the overall classroom program, see Chapter 4, which summarizes the plan-do-review process and other basic elements of the daily schedule in High/Scope classrooms and shows how science fits into this schedule.)

A third step in setting the stage for science learning is to **establish and maintain expectations for children's social behavior.** Clear expectations are, of course, a precondition for an orderly classroom in any teaching approach. However, since the High/Scope model breaks with tradition by encouraging children to work cooperatively and actively with materials, children in our classrooms may not understand what is expected of them as readily as they do in settings where "sit still and listen" is the overriding rule. Thus it is especially important for teaching adults to set expectations and maintain them consistently. Otherwise, the freedom to explore can lead to an out-of-control classroom in which no learning can take place.

Many of the rules and constraints that govern children's behavior in High/Scope classrooms grow naturally out of the way adults organize the day and the classroom to provide an orderly but stimulating environment, as will be described in Chapter 4. By planning a consistent schedule, arranging the classroom with care, and then setting clear expectations for children's behavior at different times in the daily schedule, adults prevent many management problems and make it easier to resolve conflicts when they do occur.

Developing expectations for behavior is an individual matter for each teacher and group of children; the limits and rules developed will reflect the needs and developmental levels of the children, the characteristics of the setting, and the adult's teaching style. As illustrations, we have listed below some behavioral expectations that are typical of many High/Scope classrooms:

■ Whenever possible, children get out and put away materials themselves.

■ At large-group times, children listen quietly when the teacher is talking and wait to be recognized before speaking.

■ At small-group and individual work times, natural conversation among peers and with adults is encouraged, but conversation is limited to the work at hand.

■ If a child is having difficulty with a procedure, other children are encouraged to help out if possible.

■ Children stay in their work spaces during times for individual and small-group work, except to get out and put away materials or to ask for an adult's help.

Again, the foregoing are only examples. High/Scope teachers should feel free to develop their own expectations for their own groups.

We've just discussed some first steps teachers can take to create a setting in which science activities can flourish. Next, we'll take a close look at the processes of planning science activities and working directly with children.

Planning Science Activities—Recommended Contexts

For most teachers—including both High/Scope teachers and those using more traditional approaches—the first step in planning activities is usually to select a topic for a learning experience and then think about topic-related concepts or facts to be gained from the learning experience. For example, if the general topic is the diversity of living things, the teacher might decide to promote the following concepts in a learning experience she is planning for first graders: *Animals and plants are living things and exist in many different forms; a wide variety of plants and animal forms live in the woods next to the school; some plants and animals live on land; some plants and animals live on water.*

Once the subject matter for a learning experience is selected, however, the role of the developmentally oriented teacher diverges sharply from that of the traditional teacher. Adults using a traditional teaching approach typically follow through on the selection of content by planning lectures, exercises, or other structured activities to impart the chosen concepts, and these plans often include using prepared curriculum materials. In a developmental approach, however, the task of planning learning experiences is more complex, because the teacher's role is not to transmit knowledge but to support children in discovering it. In the High/Scope teaching model, the primary ways that teachers support children's learning are (1) **by bringing children into effective contact with science materials through which they can directly experience facts and concepts** relating to the chosen topic and (2) **by promoting the science key experiences** as children work with these materials.

Children's avid interest in hunting for natural treasures can be a springboard for valuable science experiences. In "collecting" activities, children sharpen observational skills and develop their ability to classify and order materials according to their attributes and properties.

Below are discussed several contexts that involve this kind of direct experience with facts and concepts: making collections, building and designing, analyzing and testing, and making surveys. These contexts are ones that promote the key experiences.

Making Collections

Collecting activities are one valuable context for science learning that takes advantage of the avid interest most young children take in hunting for natural treasures and finding ways to preserve what they collect. Collecting encourages children to sharpen their observational skills, to notice attributes and patterns, and to classify and order materials accordingly.

For example, one teacher encouraged a group of first-graders to make a collection of leaves from plants growing near the school. This collecting excursion was the starting point for a series of activities that spanned several days. Once children had collected a large number of leaves, she asked subgroups to choose a subtask to work on, for example, sorting leaves by common shapes, sorting leaves by the shapes of their edges, and ranking the leaves by size (as measured by placing the leaves on graph paper, tracing them, and then counting the number of squares covered). She encouraged the children to communicate their findings in many ways, ranging from a simple display of leaves in a tray to leaf rubbings and spatter prints. As a follow-up to this series of activities, she planned an activity focusing on the related topic of leaves as food. Some of the concepts she covered in this activity were the following: What leaves do people eat for food? What leaves do animals eat for food? What evidence of animal eating can be seen in children's leaf collections? As part of this activity, children used the leaf collections already made and did additional collecting, both from around the school and from around their homes.

The wide range of natural materials suitable for collecting activities like this includes seeds, shells, locally grown plants, insects, sands, sea plants, soils, and rocks. The success of such activities depends up the teacher's ability to encourage purposeful observing and classifying. Some tools and materials useful for gathering, storing, and displaying collections are listed in Appendix B.

Designing and Building

Science activities that involve building and designing are a natural extension of the building that goes on in young children's play. As mentioned earlier, building experiences are valuable for young children because they allow them to explore simple physical causes. As children construct and fabricate, they also develop a greater understanding of the properties and composition of common materials. Several kinds of building activities are recommended.

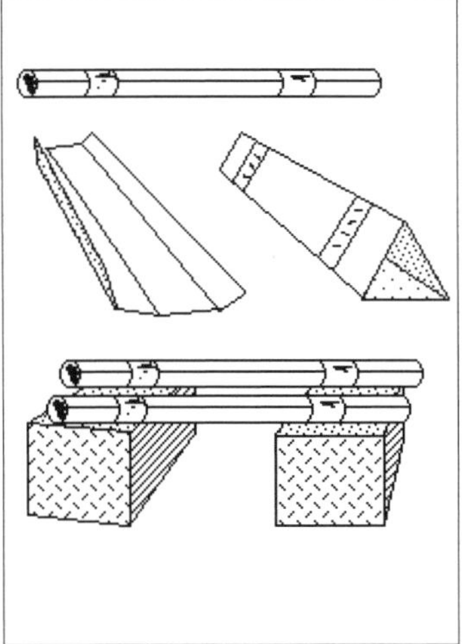

A building activity in which children design and construct girders out of rolled and folded paper and test their capacity to support loads (p. 150) is a context for exploring basic construction principles.

First, teachers can encourage children to **follow instructions to build simple mechanisms**, for example, water wheels, pinwheels, paper airplanes, parachutes, weighing devices, simple electrical devices, and so forth. In another type of activity, children **build simple structures or mechanical toys of their own design** by improvising with everyday materials; typical creations might be toy buildings or vehicles made from cardboard boxes, paper tubes, spools, long nails, wood scraps, dowels, rubber bands, foil, and so forth. Appendix B provides an extensive list of the kinds of materials that can inspire this kind of creative building. A third kind of valuable building experience occurs when teachers suggest that children **use familiar materials in new ways**. For example, children can build toy houses out of leaves, weave mats from newspaper strips, make daisy chains, construct fireplace "logs" from newspaper, make fiber ropes from long plant stems, make magnets out of pins, or use marshmallows and toothpicks to construct toy buildings. By working with materials in these unexpected ways, children develop a new understanding both of the properties of the materials they are using and of the structural features of the objects created.

Analyzing and Testing

Activities that introduce children to scientific procedures for examining materials closely and systematically are another valuable context for children's science experiences. **Analyzing** is an extension of sorting by attributes. When children analyze, they **take apart a substance or collection, note the materials that compose it, and if possible, quantify each component.** For example, children might conduct a quantitative analysis of a packet of dried fruit, a bag of bird seed, or even a bucket of litter collected from a block of city sidewalk. Typically, the first step in an analysis is identifying the different components visually, setting aside a specimen of each for identification. Next, children sort the components, and finally, they compare or measure the quantities of each component in some way. They might then discuss the implications of their findings. For example, after children have compared the quantities of raisins in boxes of two equally expensive brands of bran cereal, the teacher might ask children which brand they felt was the better buy.

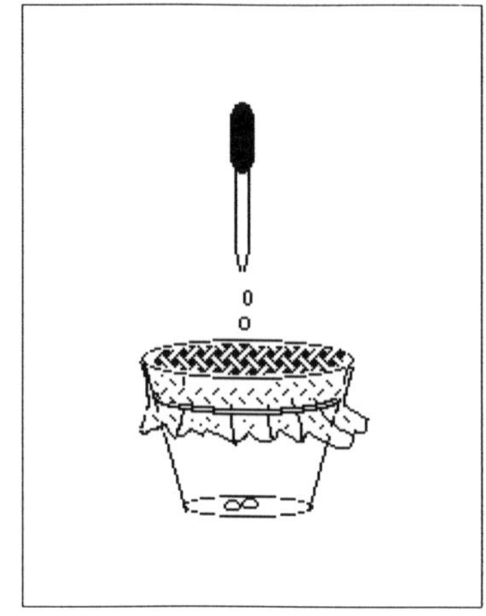

In a typical testing activity (p. 132), children use an eyedropper, squares of cloth, and waterproofing materials like crayons, candle wax, and salad oil to explore how fabrics are waterproofed and then to test and compare the effectiveness of different methods of waterproofing.

In **testing** activities, children **subject a material or an organism to a standard procedure and then assess in some systematic way the change that is produced**. For example, children could test the buoyancy of scraps of various materials (wood, cardboard, plastic foam, cork) by making small identical "rafts" of these various materials and then piling paper clips on them to see how many clips are needed to sink each type of raft.

Teachers can set the stage for some fairly complex forms of testing by carefully preparing materials beforehand as a way of controlling some of the variables involved. For example, for an activity comparing the absorbency of various materials, one teacher made several squares of fabric (e.g., cotton, nylon, wool, plastic sheeting, rainwear poplin, chamois cloth, leather), taking care to prepare samples of the same size and approximate thickness. Children placed the samples on a piece of blotting paper and tested them using an eyedropper filled with colored water. After applying a specified number of drops to each sample, the children waited three minutes. Then the teacher asked them to observe on which samples the water had soaked through to the blotting paper, how far the water spots extended on each sample, and how wet each sample felt. The teacher helped some of the children in the group to set up a numerical rating scale to code the changes observed. As a follow-up activity, she asked children to investigate the reverse process of drying the samples, using a hair dryer to speed up the process.

Testing activities like this are valuable for many reasons: They strengthen children's powers of observation, develop skills in counting and measurement, deepen children's understanding of the properties of materials, and help them understand why systematic procedures are important.

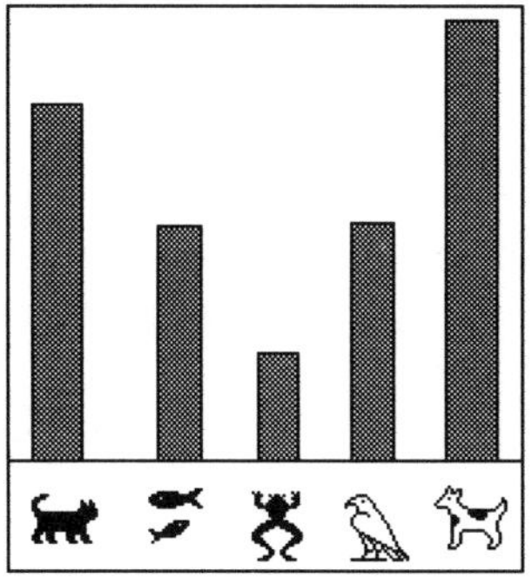

In one kind of survey activity (p. 106), children make counts of the animal life in a defined area and graph the results.

Making Surveys

Surveys are another context for science activities that children enjoy and that provide valuable experiences with important science processes. Making a survey is, in a sense, a form of collecting, since children are gathering raw materials from the immediate environment and organizing them in some way. However, the materials collected in a survey are facts or observations rather than objects or organisms; the process of organizing what is collected is one of noticing trends and inferring causes rather than one of sorting by attributes and structural patterns.

Most young children find it fascinating to **collect personal statistics from members of the group**. For example, any of the following could be the basis for a survey: ages, heights, weights, hand spans, shoe sizes, addresses, distances from home to school, model of transportation to school, hobbies, birthdays, recent books read, pets, food or color preferences.

In another kind of survey, children **make and tabulate observations about some facet of the immediate environment**, for example, roofing or siding materials used in local houses, types of bridges observed locally, wildlife or plant life seen in a given area, games played on the school playground at lunch hour, or menu items selected most often in the school cafeteria.

The value of survey activities lies in the tabulation, interpretation, and presentation of the data. At the right we present one example of graphing data collected in a survey. By helping children present information pictorially, teachers encourage them to notice trends and then to suggest explanations for these trends.

By employing such contexts as we have just described, teachers provide abundant opportunities for children to learn about the world through their own observations rather than through secondhand sources. These activity contexts offer natural and enjoyable opportunities for children to use basic science processes. We have included suggestions for many of these kinds of activities in Part 2 of this book.

Teaching Strategies

Much of the previous discussion has focused on ways to plan and structure a learning environment and classroom activities. Our teaching model also suggests certain basic strategies that teachers use as they work with children in the course of these activities.

Two general principles underlie all of planning and teaching in the High/Scope Curriculum for science. One, **the need to promote the key experiences**, has already been discussed extensively. The other guiding principle is **the need for teaching adults to share control of the learning experience with children.** The need for shared control grows from our view of learning as an active process that is individual for each child. When adults accept the view that children construct their own knowledge, they recognize that children are the principal actors in the learning process. A child cannot simply take in information and reach a new understanding without processing this new information with reference to personal goals and interests. At the same time, recognizing that learning is a child-directed process does not mean that we expect children to discover the basic concepts of science without adult input. Clearly, many of children's "discoveries" must in some sense be staged by adults. Adult involvement in children's learning activities is not only inevitable, it is desirable—as long as it is guided by a respect for the child's personal interests, individual goals, and developmental levels.

How can one insure that the principle of shared control is reflected in all of children's science experiences? Providing opportunities for children to initiate their own activities is one obvious answer to this question. For example, High/Scope's plan-do-review sequence (see Chapter 4), in which children plan and carry out a daily activity of their own choice, is one regular opportunity for child-directed science activities. But when a science activity is initiated by a teacher, as is sometimes the case, how can we assure that children have some control over the experience?

One way to encourage shared control of a teacher-initiated activity is to **encourage children to choose from among several subtasks of a suggested task or to seek solutions to an identified problem in individual ways.** For example, if a group activity focuses on using natural materials to make glue or paste, one subgroup might try to make paste with flour and water; another, with egg white and oatmeal; and another, with mud, water, and sand. Children could choose which subgroup they wanted to join and which role they wanted to play in the subgroup (e.g., measurer, mixer, note-taker, chart-maker).

Implicit in this approach is the need for adults to **avoid overprescribing the way children solve problems or complete tasks.** For instance, in the paste activity described above, the adult might not specify the quantities of materials to be used but might instead suggest that children experiment with different combinations of the materials, keeping track in some way of the proportions used. Depending on the children's levels of development, the end result of this activity might be a recipe expressed in precise terms ("Two cups flour plus one cup water makes the stickiest paste"), a simple observation ("If the paste gets too watery, it doesn't stick"), or a recipe expressed in descriptive, rather than quantitative terms, ("Keep adding water to the flour and stir until the paste is smooth and about this thick"). In an approach that allows children to carry out tasks in their own way, teachers are ready to accept results that differ from one another, since children invariably see problems differently and work at them at different levels. If the teacher provides exact instructions in a task like this, the children may achieve results that are more perfect by adult standards. But they may also be so busy carrying out instructions that they do not expand their understanding of the properties of the materials involved.

Developmental teaching recognizes that different children will be at different points in their development at any one point in time. It also recognizes that children with differing working concepts and interests will follow different paths as they seek solutions to the same problems. Allowing and encouraging this diversity is a hallmark of developmental teaching. Effecting it requires striking a balance between teacher contributions and child contributions to any given learning situation. A hallmark of teaching that is not developmentally oriented is the appearance of "perfect" and identical creations from all children.

Another primary way that teachers encourage a balance between teacher and child input to the learning experience is to **involve children in instructional dialogue**. In contrast to lecturing or correcting children or, at the other extreme, allowing children to work on their own without any adult intervention, instructional dialogue is a conversation between child and teacher about what the child is doing, about the child's goal for the activity, and about ways to reach that goal. As in any real conversation, the communication is two-way. The teacher is sensitive to the direction taken by the child and to the child's inherent abilities. Yet it is also important for the teacher to offer information, draw out the child, and help him or her elaborate on the work he or she has undertaken. Often this can be accomplished by *asking questions* in a kind of Socratic dialogue. At other times, the best way to support a child is *by listening to or observing him or her* and then *suggesting materials or techniques* that may help with the task he or she has in mind. Sometimes, *introducing a new challenge or extension to a task* can be the key to helping the child reach a new level of understanding. Conversations of this kind are the main way that teachers promote the key experiences as children work independently. The example at the right illustrates how both adults and children contribute to instructional dialogue.

Implicit in our description of the processes both of planning for children's activities and of supporting them as they work is the need to **identify the child's level of performance relative to the overall scope of elementary science development.** Again, the key experiences serve as the guide for teachers as they identify levels of development. For example, if a child has collected a group of fall leaves and is busy sorting the collection by color, the teacher familiar with the key experiences will recognize that this is one of the most basic kinds of sorting possible. It may be possible for the teacher to encourage the child to move to a more complex form of sorting, for example, to re-sort the leaves by their general shapes, or by the shapes of the edges, or by the presence or absence of evidence of insect damage. These activities would require the child to notice additional attributes of the leaves and to shift the criteria for sorting. In introducing such additional challenges, the teacher has recognized the level

Involving Children in Instructional Dialogue

A class of second-graders has been studying bridges, both in the environment and in a series of workshop experiences planned around exploring various ways to bridge a gap. On this day, the teacher has supplied a small group with dominoes, opening the workshop with this question: "Can you use these to make an arch or a bridge?

After the children have worked for a few minutes, most have discovered how to build a bridge with one domino spanning the gap.

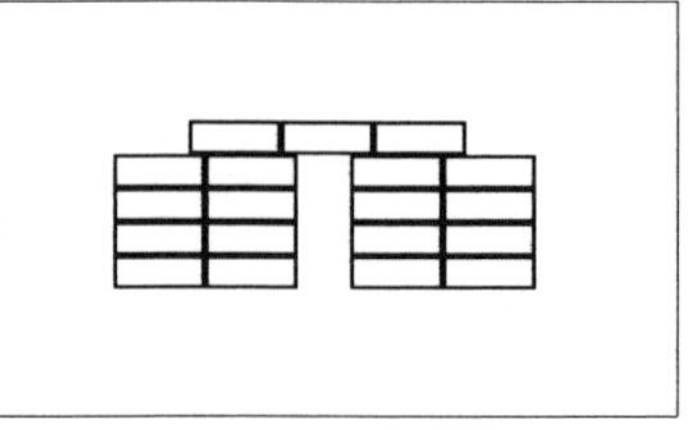

The teacher then says, "You've figured out one good way to bridge the gap. Can anybody figure out how to make a bridge over an opening that's wider than one domino?" (This is only possible by counterbalancing the dominoes that are bridging the gap with other dominoes on the outside of the arch, i.e., by building a cantilevered arch.)

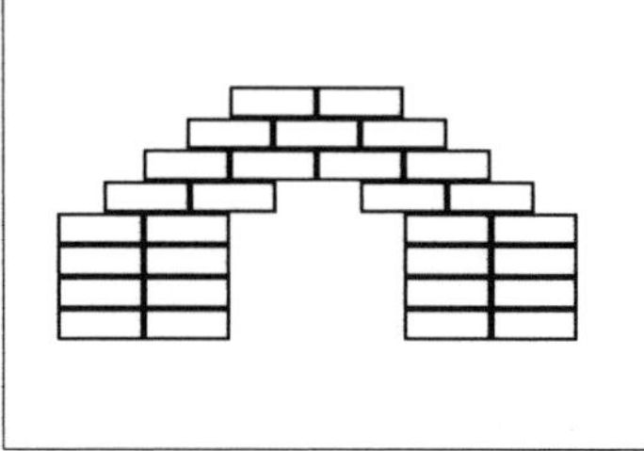

Observing Tommy's successful solution, the teacher says, "I see you found a way

of the child's performance and suggested a level of effort a bit higher. This process of identifying the child's performance relative to the overall sequence of science processes is essential to the dialogue that the teacher has with the child at work.

to make the opening bigger! How did you get that to work?"

"Well, you have to have some blocks on the outside to balance it," Tommy answers.

The teacher responds, "So you've found that it's balance that makes this work." ■

When to Intervene: Stages in Problem Solving

In an approach that strives to balance the roles of children and adults in shaping the learning experience, sensitive timing of adult intervention is critical. A conceptual framework that may be useful in helping adults know *when* to intervene in children's work is to think of classroom activities in terms of five stages in problem solving. Each of these stages represents a transition point at which adult support may enhance the child's learning. We've listed the five stages in the chart that follows. With each stage, we've listed possible support strategies that adults may use at that stage.

All the strategies listed in our chart are possible ways to keep the problem-solving process moving along. The fact that each stage offers opportunities for adult input, however, does not mean that teachers *should* always intervene. Instead, the developmentally oriented teacher allows the child to take the lead and waits for the "right moment" before intervening. Sometimes this moment comes when children are stuck or discouraged and may benefit from a clarification, a new material, or a new technique. Another good time to step in may be a moment of success. When children's enthusiasm is running high, they can be encouraged to consolidate what they have learned by stating or graphing their findings or to take on a new challenge that builds on what they have learned.

On the pages immediately following the chart, we present an extended example that illustrates a teacher's sensitive intervention in the problem-solving process. In the right-hand column of each of these pages, we have noted the support strategies and key experiences the teacher is using in each instance of intervention. Notice how restrained this teacher is in guiding children's work. When children have a problem, she allows them to struggle for a while before stepping in, and then she provides only as much information as is needed to encourage the children to continue their explorations.

Stages in Problem-Solving: Appropriate Support Strategies

1. The child recognizes that there is a problem, defines some elements of it, and makes a commitment to solve it.

Possible support strategies:

- Present materials that suggest problems.
- Help the child recognize that a problem exists.
- Help the child define and state the problem.
- Encourage the child to make a decision to solve the problem.

2. The child examines the problem and collects information (from other experiences, from the environment, etc.) that may bear on solving it.

Possible support strategies:

- Remind the child of relevant concepts, information, experiences that bear on the problem.
- Offer new techniques, materials, facts that may be helpful.
- Encourage the child to search actively for additional information that may be relevant to solving the problem.

3. The child analyzes the total information now available and structures it into possible plans for a solution.

Possible support strategies:

- Point out relationships among facts and concepts that will help the child use the total information available to develop plans leading to a possible solution.
- Encourage the child to state possible solutions.

4. The child selects for trial the plan that appears most promising from among the various possibilities. The child uses the selected plan to attack the problem.

Possible support strategies:

- Encourage the child to consider factors that may affect the feasibility of the proposed solutions.
- Encourage the child to risk failure and test out a possible solution.

5. The child assesses the effectiveness of the plan. If a satisfactory solution has been achieved, it is regarded as a result. If not, the child analyzes and modifies the original plan, and the cycle is repeated.

Possible support strategies:

If the trial has been successful . . .

- Encourage children to represent their findings in some way: by stating them verbally, by graphing them, or by listing them.
- Encourage children to apply their findings in a new context.
- Suggest modifications that use the same basic plan but make it more workable.
- Suggest a related challenge or extension to the task.

If the trial has proven unsuccessful . . .

- Encourage children to discuss what didn't work and why.
- Encourage children to generate additional possible solutions and to risk failure again by trying them out.
- Remind children of their original plan and encourage them to persist in their efforts to solve the problem.

An Extended Example: Working Through the Problem-Solving Process

A group of third-grade children were interested in electric lighting. After a discussion with the children, the teacher provided them with lengths of wire, bulbs in bulb holders, and a battery, saying "Here are the things you asked for. Now you can make the lights."

⇐ **Support strategy:** Present materials that suggest problems.

⇐ **Key experience:** Building with electrical circuits.

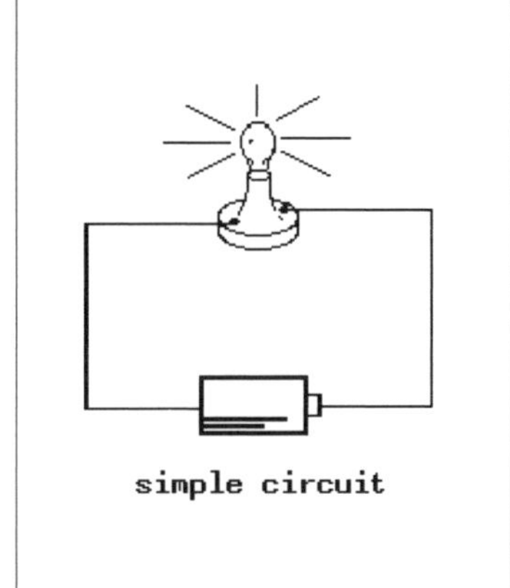

simple circuit

There was no doubt about the children's interest in and acceptance of the problem posed by the teacher. They immediately proceeded with attempts to make the light come on. Some perceived at once that connections were needed and made various attempts to link bulb holders with the battery, but with no success. It was apparent to the children that the contact screws on the bulb holders had a purpose—but the insulated wire was difficult to secure, and the circuits they devised were not the correct ones.

Seeing the children had come to a point where intervention was vital to maintain their interest and the momentum of the work, the teacher stepped in to show the children that the insulation had to be removed from the wire. She offered a set of wires from which the end insulation had been removed and whose ends had been bent into a hook shape to go around the contact screws.

⇐ **Support strategy:** Offer a new technique or material.

The children again began working enthusiastically, and after many trial-and-error operations, they finally got the light working. Their exclamations of success brought the teacher back to observe the group. To relieve the children who were holding the contacts in place by hand, she suggested tightening the connections by screwing down the screws leading to the battery and the bulb holder.

⇐ **Key experience:** Improving a structure or material through trial-and-error modifications.

⇐ **Support strategy:** Offer a new technique.

The teacher then suggested the children draw up a plan of the circuit they had made, so others could follow it to make their own working lights.

⇐ **Key experience:** Using models, drawings, or diagrams to illustrate oral or written reports.

The teacher's suggestion raised a new problem: The children realized the battery would run down if the light remained on while they were busy drawing. How would they switch if off? One member of the group soon settled the issue by removing a wire from the battery, and the children proceeded with their drawings. The teacher returned to the group and asked them how they had turned the light off. When they told her, the teacher immediately saw the chance to ask "What will make the light come on again?"

⇐ **Support strategy:** Suggest a related challenge or extension to a task.

Another member of the group quickly reconnected the circuit, making the light come on. The teacher then left the group with this problem: Were there other ways to switch the light off? The group experimented with disconnecting and reconnecting all the other connection points (gaining skill with the screwdriver in the process).

The teacher returned to observe the group. They had become absorbed in the task of making a flashing light by touching the battery terminal with the bare wire, which they had straightened to make this easier. She looked at their drawings of the circuit and entered a dialogue in which she encouraged them to state one of the fundamentals they had discovered: A continuous wire circuit is necessary for the bulb to light; when there is a gap in the route, the light goes out. *She then extended on this dialogue by suggesting that the children try to invent a switch.*

⇐ **Support strategy:** Encourage children to represent their findings.

⇐ **Key experience:** Observing and describing a pattern of change.

⇐ **Support strategy:** Suggest a related challenge or extension to a task.

The teacher walked away, leaving the children debating about how to make a switch. She suggested they call her if they needed help finding materials. (She knew they would, but wisely left the debate to the children.) The group tried many types of bent wires in efforts to make a switch. Stuck, they went to the teacher.

"Would these help?" the teacher asked, offering them some blocks of wood, thumbtacks, and long paper clips.

⇐ **Support strategy:** Offer a new material.

The teacher stayed with the group as they viewed the materials with bewilderment. The problem of relating these items to their new knowledge of circuits seemed almost beyond their abilities. She referred them back to their discovery that it is a gap in the path that breaks the circuit and makes the light go out, and when the circuit is restored the light goes on. Then she put one thumbtack into the end of the paper clip and pressed it into the wooden block, saying "Will this help?"

⇐ **Support strategy:** Encourage children to apply their findings in a new context.

⇐ **Support strategy:** Offer a new technique.

With surprising persistence, the group continued their efforts to invent a switch. After much discussion and manipulation, they finally succeeded. They realized that connections could be made under the thumbtacks and that a second thumbtack made the second contact they needed.

The switch was made and tested in the circuit. It worked! The teacher encouraged the children to make a new drawing showing the switch to the circuit.

⇐ **Support strategy**: Encourage children to represent their findings.

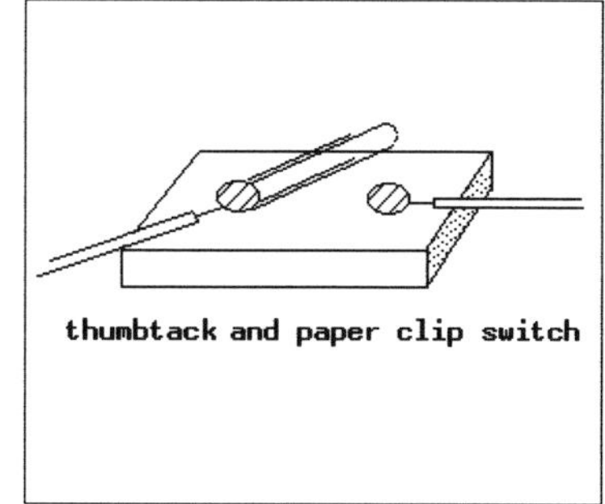

thumbtack and paper clip switch

The next day, the children were still excited over their triumphs with circuits. The teacher suggested a follow-up activity: Could they make satisfactory bulb holders that functioned in their simple circuits? The children struggled with this problem, and the teacher encouraged them to stick with the task. Eventually there were successful outcomes. A few of these are illustrated here. With the children's enthusiasm about their experiments with electricity still running high, the teacher decided to carry over the activity for several more days. She felt children should know that their problem solving and the associated inventions had a purpose beyond just the replication of effects. Thus she stressed that the real purpose of a lighting circuit is to do a job: to provide lights for a house, a car, a signal. She suggested that children construct applications for simple circuitry. The classroom had a big stack of cardboard boxes of all kinds and a large supply of construction "junk," so there was no shortage of materials for improvisation. Some results of this work are shown in the illustrations on the next page.

⇐ **Support strategy:** Suggest a related challenge or extension to a task.

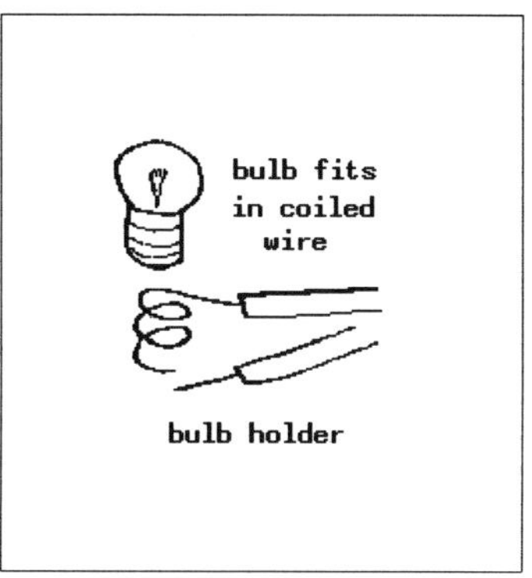

bulb holder

⇐ **Support strategy:** Encourage children to apply their findings in a new context.

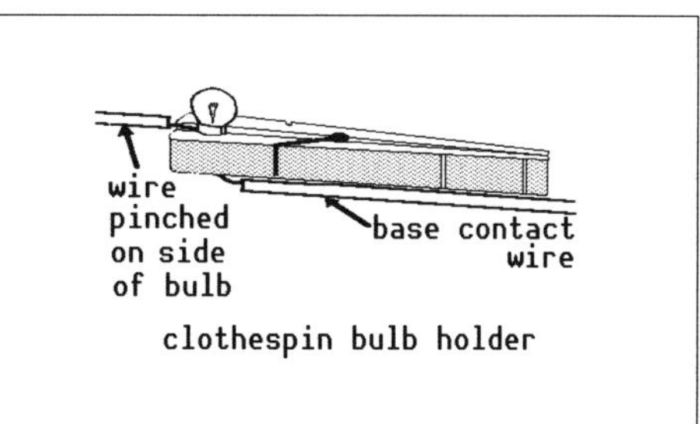

clothespin bulb holder

Sometimes teachers sense they are nearing the limits of children's conceptual range but feel it is appropriate to prod children to extend these limits. This teacher knew that the topic of series and parallel circuits would tax these third-graders, but she saw the opportunity to introduce the subject when discussing the traffic light circuits several children had constructed. The children had powered each of the two circuits with a separate battery. The teacher asked, "Do you think you could run the traffic lights with only one battery? Could this be done without dimming the power of the lights?"

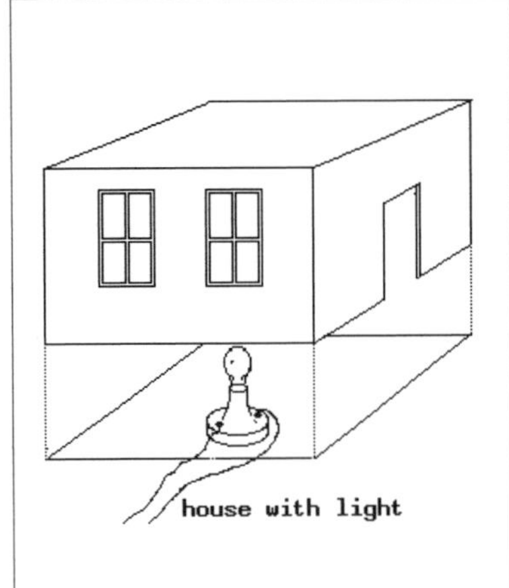

⇐ **Support strategy**: Suggest a new challenge or extension to a task.

This proved to be a problem too great for the children to solve unaided, because it required either two switches or another type of switch that could be used to alternate the red and green lights. When the teacher perceived this problem was beyond the children's present limits, she decided that if she intervened further, the work would cease to be the children's. Wisely, she changed tack to set a different problem in context: Could the group power two car headlights from one battery and control this with one switch? She showed the group that the egg boxes could be used as headlights if they were placed horizontally instead of vertically. By experimenting, the group discovered two ways of wiring the circuit (series and parallel). One type of circuit used less wiring but gave less light; the other used more wiring but gave two good bright lights.

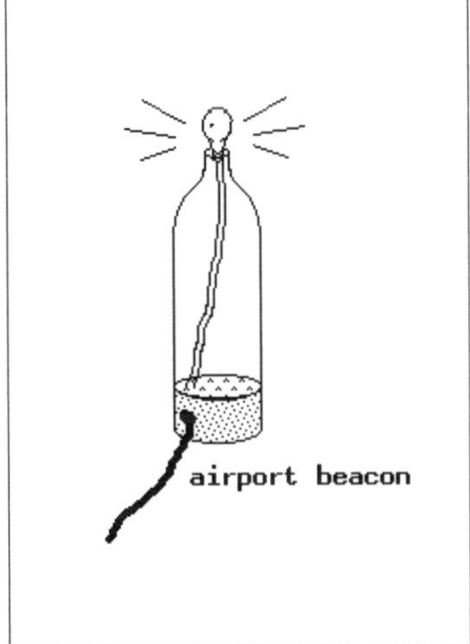

⇐ **Support strategy**: Follow the children's lead.

⇐ **Support strategy:** Suggest a new challenge or extension to a task.

bulbs covered with colored cellophane

egg carton traffic light

This was a difficult problem that these children solved with a minimum of teacher assistance. The main way the teacher helped out was (once the circuits were discovered) by bending wires so it was easier to connect the wires with the bulb holders.

⇐ **Support strategy**: Once a solution is found to a problem, suggest modifications that use the same basic plan but make it more workable.

This last instance is typical of much of the help that teachers are called on to give during young children's build-

ing activities. At this stage, children need as much help with manipulative skills as they do with reasoning skills. Children's construction ambitions often outrun their skill in producing their designs. In these cases, the teacher can often help ameliorate such problems by suggesting alternative materials or, as in this instance, by suggesting an improvement once the basic design is in order (assuming that children want assistance).

* * * * *

This example illustrates why the dialogue between teacher and child is so vital to the child's problem-solving process. In activities like these, teachers assist children's active learning by setting up the situation, providing the right materials at the right time, and highlighting opportunities for learning as the activity unfolds.

The example focuses on one teacher's experience in applying the High/Scope science key experiences and teaching strategies with her particular group of children. Another teacher might have found a different but equally valid way to approach the same subject matter. The High/Scope approach is an "open framework" whose application depends on the teacher's individual style and the needs of the children he or she is working with. For additional "real-life" examples of teachers' experiences in using this approach, see Chapter 5.

Assessing Children's Science Experiences

Assessment is an important part of science teaching because it helps teachers gauge individual students' progress and generates feedback that helps teachers plan further science experiences. Assessment also contributes to overall program evaluation.

In planning assessment methods for science, teachers often have more freedom than they have in other curriculum areas in which pressures for achievement testing are sometimes stronger. This freedom creates an opportunity for teachers to devise unique assessment plans that are tailored to the needs of their programs.

In deciding how to assess science activities, teachers must first consider the compatibility of assessment methods with the goals, emphases, instructional approach, and content of High/Scope Curriculum programs. In light of the curriculum's emphasis on hands-on science experiences and process-oriented learning, most teachers find that paper-and-pencil tests are not a useful way to evaluate individual children's progress or the program as a whole. It is up to each teacher to find the combination of assessment techniques that works best for him or her. Some alternative assesment techniques that teachers in High/Scope programs have found useful are discussed below.

Observation and Note-taking

Observing closely what children do and say and keeping some kind of anecdotal records of these observations are essential elements of assessment in programs that emphasize experience-based learning. Notes may be jotted down on cards or small notepads that are kept available at all times, or they may be typed in a computer-based file; whatever system is used, the notes should be brief, nonjudgmental records of what children have done, focusing on strengths and small achievments rather than on deficits. For example, during an activity in which children compare the ways different kinds of balls bounce on different surfaces, a teacher might note: "Athi pointed out that balls bounced higher on the hard floor than on the rug. He also suggested that the small, hard balls bounced higher than the big, soft balls."

We recommend that teachers use the science key experiences to help them interpret their observations. For example, with reference to the key experiences, the above report on Athi's behavior suggests that Athi is beginning to realize more than one cause can influence the outcome of an event. The key experiences are also helpful to teachers in planning what to look for when they observe children. For example, a teacher who has planned an activity in which children will be measuring changes might look for the following dimensions of children's behavior suggested by the key experiences in measurement and in understanding causality: Can children use measurement units, or are they assessing effects only by comparison? Are they comparing intuitively or systematically? Are they making guesses about the causes of the changes they measure or compare? Are any children considering the possibility that more than one cause could be involved in producing the changes observed? Are any children able to relate the magnitude of the change produced to the magnitude of a causal factor?

Observation Checklists

If teachers are accustomed to using the key experiences to frame their observations, an observation checklist based on the key experiences can be helpful in recording observations. Appendix A provides such a checklist. Using the checklist systematically, in conjunction with regular observation and note-taking, provides a useful gauge of the development of a child's scientific thinking and problem solving.

Case Histories

Case histories like those presented in Chapter 5 are another form of anecdotal record. Case histories document the planning and implementation of a science activity or series of activities. First, teachers note the particulars of the activity they are planning: the materials to be used, and the concepts, processes, and problems they expect that children will be working with. Later, they document what actually happened. As they review an activity afterwards, they will often find that it unfolded in unexpected directions. This kind of detailed record of a classroom experience can be useful in many ways: it helps teachers plan further, related experiences for the same group of children, or similar experiences for a different group of children; it also can provide an illustration of the teacher's approach for parents, administrators, or other interested outsiders.

Work Samples

Nearly all the science activities presented in this book include suggestions for children to document their experience in some way: by producing graphs, displays, reports, charts, and so on. Saving child-made work samples such as these in children's individual portfolios assures children that their work is valued and important, and helps document children's achievements and progress. Work samples have such an important role to play in documenting an experience-based curriculum that we urge teachers to use creativity in their attempts to capture children's classroom experiences in permanent ways. For example, a teacher could photograph or videotape the various stages of a bridge-building activity, or make an audio tape of a child's description of the collapse of a bridge he constructed. Such teacher-made work samples could also be filed in children's personal portfolios, or they could be displayed or shared at parent open houses as an illustration of the work of the whole group.

In this chapter, we've explained the techniques teachers use for planning, carrying out, and assessing developmentally-based science activities. In the next chapter we turn to classroom management, offering suggestions for structuring the daily schedule, arranging the classroom, and gathering materials for science learning.

4

Classroom Management and Science Materials

In the High/Scope classroom, the daily schedule and the environment are carefully planned to encourage activity-based learning in all areas of the curriculum. The classroom is stocked with a wide array of materials that invite exploration and discovery. Many of the materials used for science learning are stocked in a "science area," one of several activity areas that are used for children's independent work or for small-group activities. Following are some general guidelines for scheduling science work, planning a science area, and collecting science materials.

Classroom Management

The approach to science learning presented in this book is intended to fit within High/Scope's overall guidelines for classroom management. A key feature of this approach is a daily schedule that includes times for small- and large-group activities in various content areas and also time for an individual project time—the plan-do-review time—in which children plan an activity of their own choice, carry it out, and then record and share the results with others. Opportunities for children to make choices and initiate activities are emphasized throughout the day, as well, even during group activities.

Science Activities in the Daily Schedule

Time periods devoted to science will vary from one classroom to another, based on the constraints of the overall school schedule. Here we explain some basic considerations for scheduling science work and offer two examples of how elementary teachers using the High/Scope Curriculum have arranged their schedules for science activities.

It is assumed that the developmentally-oriented teacher who is using this book will already have in place a daily schedule that allots time both for children's independent work in activity areas and for teacher-led instructional activities in large or small groups. A typical sample of one such first-grade schedule is given at the right.

Note that the sample schedule provides several opportunities for science experiences. The science/social studies block is devoted to science two to three times per week. These science sessions may be used either for whole-group or small-group activities. In whole-group times, science concepts may be introduced or the whole class may participate in a science activity, for example, a collecting excursion on the school grounds. Many science activities (e.g., an introduction to the planting of seeds or to a new science computer program) can be efficiently accomplished in such a large-group setting. The large-group activities can lead to follow-up activities for small groups in subsequent science/social studies blocks. Or, small-group science experiments may be integrated with other academic areas, occurring, for example, during math or language workshop times.

Children may also follow up on large- or small-group science activities during their time for independent work, the plan-do-review time. The plan-do-review time is a device the High/Scope Curriculum uses to organize children's independent work in activity areas. Once a science area has been established, it is one of children's options for their independent work time. For example, soon after magnets have been introduced during a whole-group session, they may be used in a subsequent small-group science activity and then placed in the science area for independent exploration. Several students might then choose, during plan-do review time, to use the magnets to search out and chart magnetic and nonmagnetic materials in the classroom.

Sample First-Grade Daily Schedule

8:30–8:50
Opening

8:50–9:10
Music

9:10–10:30
Math workshop

10:30–10:40
Story time

10:40–11:10
Whole-group reading

11:10–12:10
Language workshop

12:10–12:35
Lunch

12:35–1:05
Science/social studies

1:05–1:30
Physical education

1:30–2:50
Plan-do-review time (independent work time)

2:50
Dismissal

As we've already mentioned, one way of scheduling science work is to use a workshop period for multiple small groups to work simultaneously on similar or different tasks. The aim of this is to maximize opportunities for children to interact with materials. For example, each small group could work on making a chart, graph, model, or apparatus. Small groups allow efficient utilization of limited classroom resources such as computers, balances, or spring scales. Sufficient materials can be provided so each child or pair of children in a small group can work with them directly. The teacher presents a task to each group and provides the materials; each child (or pair of children) approaches the task in an individual way.

The sample at the right, a second-grade teacher's daily schedule, shows one way to schedule science activities. During the math/science workshop time in this second-grade classroom, four small groups of youngsters alternate tasks, as shown in the sidebar on the next page. As can be seen, one of the small-group activities offered during this workshop period has a science focus. During the workshop time, the teacher devotes the majority of his or her attention to one of the small groups. Other small groups work more independently, though the teacher is available to help them if the need arises. The use of workshop time is intended to be flexible. If, for example, the teacher wishes to introduce a concept to the group as a whole, half the workshop time on a particular day can be allotted for a whole-class activity.

If at least one of the teacher-led workshop activities per week is devoted to science, approximately 30 science activities can be introduced throughout the year during a normal school schedule. In addition, child-chosen science activities may take place during plan-do-review times.

Representation and communication are central to the process of science and should have clearly defined places in the daily schedule. A working model, picture, chart, or written report should be the expected outcome of nearly all science experiences. Sharing of these representations with other members of the class may take place during a review period at the end of the day or at some other time. Models and other representations can be kept on display in the science area or in a display space inside or outside the classroom.

Sample Second-Grade Daily Schedule

8:30–8:40
Opening

8:40–9:30
Whole-group reading

9:30–10:00
Language workshop

10:00–10:30
Physical education

10:30–11:20
Continuation of language workshop

11:20–11:30
Clean up

11:30–11:50
Music (M,W), art (T,Th,F)

11:50–12:45
Plan-do-review time

12:45–1:15
Lunch

1:15–1:30
Story time

1:30–2:30
Math/science workshop

2:30–2:50
Clean up & review of day

Classroom Layout

The furniture, materials, and physical layout of the classroom set the stage for science activities. The scheduling guidelines just given and considerations for selecting materials that will follow can help in establishing science as a significant part of your classroom.

The general organization of the classroom supports active learning by providing materials for exploration, supplies for creative projects, and appropriate work areas. The classroom is designed to respond to the differing and changing interests of the children. Activity areas that are well stocked with materials provide many options for children to express their interests and to initiate projects of their own, including those relating directly to science.

In addition to specific science materials, the classroom as a whole provides opportunities and resources for science experiences. A sink and water supply provides material for working with fluids. General classroom supplies provide a variety of plastic, wood, metal, cloth, and other materials suitable for children's collections or for building and construction projects.

Planning the science area

The science area is typically one of five or six activity areas in the classroom. A well-planned science area reflects the various aspects of science work and includes—preferably close by one another—a space for active work with science materials, a space for displays and collections, and a space for books and other secondary resources. (In some classrooms, it may be more practical to locate books or extra display shelves in a space that is not contiguous with the actual work area.)

Space to work and explore. A clearly defined and labeled work area is basic for classroom science experiences. This area need not be large: a table and nearby storage shelf will suffice. Locating the area fairly close to the classroom water supply is helpful but not necessary; also helpful is a nearby electrical outlet for plugging in lamps, fans, and other electrical equipment and for recharging batteries.

Space to observe and display. Providing display and storage space is important for classroom projects in general and especially important for science projects. A class-

Sample Math/ Science Workshop Schedule

Group 1

1:30–1:45 computers
1:45–2:00 math 1
2:00–2:15 math 2
2:15–2:30 science

Group 2

1:30–1:45 math 1
1:45–2:00 math 2
2:00–2:15 science
2:15–2:30 computers

Group 3

1:30–1:45 math 2
1:45–2:00 science
2:00–2:15 computers
2:15–2:30 math 1

Group 4

1:30–1:45 science
1:45–2:00 computers
2:00–2:15 math 1
2:15–2:30 math 2

room may have a permanent general display area: a bulletin board, shelf, or tabletop. It is also helpful to provide a shelf or two specifically in the science area for special-interest displays. An area close to a window may be needed for growing seeds and plants. If you are sure that ideal living conditions can be provided for small animals, space might also be provided for cages, where children can care for mice, guinea pigs, rabbits, baby chicks, or other living creatures. (An alternative is having such animals as classroom visitors.)

Some teachers like to have two display areas, one for work in progress and one for finished work. During review time, ongoing work can be on temporary display—e.g., a half-finished chart can be pinned up for discussion, or an apparatus under construction can be moved to a table where children are discussing the day's work. A smaller, general-purpose space will probably be adequate for such temporary displays, but as large a display area as possible is needed for finished products. Even in classrooms where display space is limited and all shelves and tabletops are needed for other uses, some wall space is usually available. Charts, graphs, and posters, of course, are easily displayed on walls. Many collections, suitably mounted, can also be hung on walls.

Many kinds of charts, graphs, photos, and collections need to be mounted to make effective displays. Keeping a stock of old picture frames (without glass) on hand can provide a quick and effective means of presenting finished work without the trouble of cutting mounts. Double-sided cellophane tape or poster tape will hold the work in place. Good communication depends on good labeling to carry its message. Some children have good lettering skills, but for others, this can be a burden. In these cases, stencils, press-on letters, or labels made with a computer or word processor can provide effective alternatives.

For classrooms with very limited wall space, folding, accordion-type display units can be made to increase the available surface for hanging displays. Folding units can also be used for open houses or other special events, when extra displays are expected. To make a folding

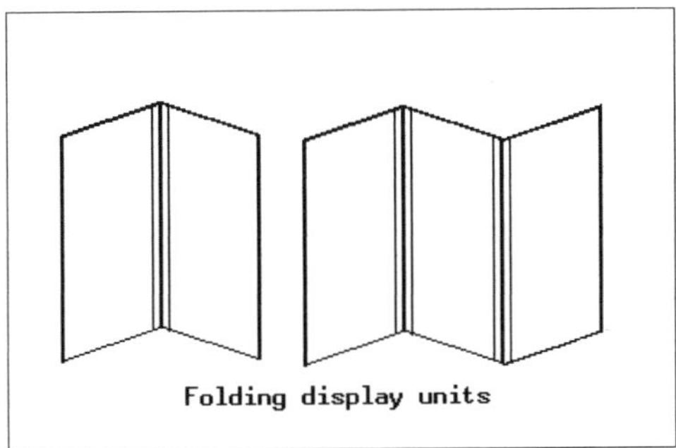
Folding display units

display unit, simply connect several thick cardboard or hardboard sheets so they fold at the joints. Use wide tape to join the sheets, being sure to allow for easy folding by leaving between-sheet gaps that are slightly wider than the thickness of the cardboard. Tape the joints back and front to strengthen them. Large and small versions of this design can be made for tabletop displays.

Sometimes, efforts to communicate results may extend beyond the immediate classroom. Display spaces in corridors or on corridor walls can provide a useful public outlet for science work. Such opportunities for public display can also spur children to improve the quality of their efforts.

Space to reflect and read. We do not expect that primary-grade children will gain all their science knowledge through interaction with "hands-on" materials, though this process is especially important to science. Books on science, scientists, and events in science are also important for young children's science learning. Books stimulate interest in science and are also a source of science activities. Equally important, reading material in science can help to integrate science with other curriculum areas, such as reading and writing.

Science books, magazines, and guides may be placed in the classroom library along with other books, but at least some space should be reserved in the science area for topical books related to subjects under study and for resource guides and picture books that may stimulate science activities. (See the activities in Part 2 for lists of suggested books on various topics.)

Storing materials for independent use

To facilitate children's independent science activities in the High/Scope classroom, it is essential that materials be in easy reach of children and in clearly labeled containers or on labeled shelves. This not only saves teachers the trouble of getting materials out, it also creates a problem-solving situation in which children learn to take care of their own needs. Children quickly become accustomed to choosing tools and materials, getting them out, using them independently, working out ways to share them, if necessary, and, finally, putting them away. The expectation that materials will be handled independently is easier to establish if the children have been to a High/Scope preschool, where such routines are part of the program. If the children have not had such experiences, it may take some time, but teachers can convey this new approach by clearly explaining expectations, modeling appropriate procedures, and consistently encouraging children to handle materials independently.

There are jobs, of course, that an adult must help with, for example, drilling holes, cutting thick materials, or handling heavy buckets of water. Children should know that an adult is available to give such help. Sometimes, too, children need to acquire certain manipulative skills to handle science tools and apparatus. In this case, the teacher should be ready to model the correct procedure. Some skills—for example, using an electrician's screwdriver and small screws—can be readily learned; other procedures—such as making scales for measurement—may require several teacher interventions. If children are working in a group, adults can encourage those children who have a skill to demonstrate it to others, thus encouraging the development of cooperative work skills.

Of course, storage of materials must be carefully planned to assure that children can use them independently. A first consideration is that science materials should be at children's eye level. Containers should be ones that they can handle easily. Adults should look for inexpensive, stackable containers that fit the space available and are not too large for children to handle. Strong cardboard boxes will suffice for this purpose and are usually easily obtained, though teachers should avoid departing from a chosen brand, as differences in size and strength can create problems. Wooden crates set on wheels also make useful storage units, with the advantage that children can pull them out as they are needed. Again, labeling of all boxes and storage units is important.

Materials of general use in the classroom but also of use in science, such as paper and scissors, will obviously have their own storage places, but it is helpful to place these near the science area, if possible. Paper, writing tools, and other supplies for making displays may pose problems of orderly storage and economical use. This can be partly overcome if a separate "communication area" is set up containing the paper, poster-making supplies, tape recorders, and so forth. Some teachers have found an old chest of drawers ideal for such a storage unit.

Measuring tools, such as rulers, scales, and balances, are likely to be stored in a math area, as are collections of small manipulative materials (e.g., shells, nuts, bolts, and washers) and sorting trays. In general there will be considerable overlap between science and mathematics materials. When space is at a premium, special science materials can be placed in a "math and science area."

Some schools that have space in corridors, but not in classrooms, have solved storage problems by placing science supplies on two or three carts that they park in the corridor and wheel into the room when needed. The materials are stored in cardboard boxes, just as in conventional science areas. In theory, one set of carts so placed could service two or three classrooms, but in our experience, this is rarely successful, for several reasons. First, each class has its own schedule and style of working; second, shared equipment tends to be no one's real responsibility; and third, children need to know, and see, the supplies they and their classmates are responsible for. Teachers, too, like to keep tabs on just what is in stock, and this is hard to do when other groups are also using the supplies.

Providing for Safety

No discussion of classroom management is complete without a mention of safety considerations. The teacher must keep safety in mind at all times during science activities. As a general rule, we suggest that if an activity requires special safety precautions, do not undertake it. Other general guidelines: If children work with sources of heat, restrict them to warm water, heat from a radiator, or the sun. Never use naked flames of any sort. Avoid having children themselves plug things in; use battery power whenever possible for electrical experiments. (Note: To avoid waste, use rechargeable batteries, recharged by the teacher.)

Prevent accidents by selecting and preparing materials carefully. Use plastic containers instead of glass. If rough metal edges are left on materials, file them smooth. If glass must be used, as with mirrors, back it with tape. Use clear plastic when transparent glass is needed. When children will be using tools, instruct them in the correct use of the tool and the selection of the right tool for the job. School policies on what tools children can use will vary; in general, however, children may work independently with hammers, screwdrivers for electrical connections, files, and pliers; but when making holes, either with bradawls or drills, they should have direct teacher supervision.

Extra vigilance may be needed on outdoor excursions, especially when you work with children near water or on building sites. Prevent management problems by explaining limits for children's behavior beforehand and by providing challenging tasks that give children something to do besides watch and wait. If the assigned task is to observe, make the observation active by encouraging children to observe with a specific focus: to quantify their observations, to take notes, to make tape recordings or take photos, and so forth. When activities spring from children's genuine interests or from exciting possibilities brought into focus by the teacher, children are less likely to get caught up in horseplay that could lead to accidents.

Selection of Materials for Science Learning

Many people associate science work with racks of test tubes, complicated electronics, or other specialized equipment. Yet many great scientific discoveries have been made by observing commonplace phenomena or by using apparatus built from everyday materials. Highly technical equipment and materials are not needed to convey the concepts of elementary-level science. Simple phenomena created with everyday materials can be the source of great discoveries for children, especially since these are often first-time experiences. The sense of wonder sparked by such experiences can motivate children to further efforts, but their enthusiasm can be dampened by a pedantic insistence on the "right things" being used. For example, consider the use of comparative measurement. Lengths of string can be just as good as a tape measure to assess differences in length, if all you need to know, at a particular stage, is which object is longest or shortest. If, at a later stage, you need to know the exact difference, then conventional measurement may be used. In the former case, the children using the string experience the excitement of quickly seeing the result, not the frustration of reading the tape measure to the nearest fraction of a unit.

Thus in planning science activities, both children and teachers need to ask (1) What is available? and (2) How can I use this to help solve the problem? More often than not, the result of this process will be the realization that everyday materials will suffice for the purpose at hand. Such materials can be used in a variety of ways. For example, a plastic detergent bottle can be a lighthouse in one context, a rain gauge in another (see illustrations), or a musical instrument in still another (if partly filled with dried peas). To aid teachers in collecting materials for science activities, Appendix B lists a wide range of appropriate materials—most of which are inexpensive, everyday items. Many "found" materials that parents and children can assist in collecting are included.

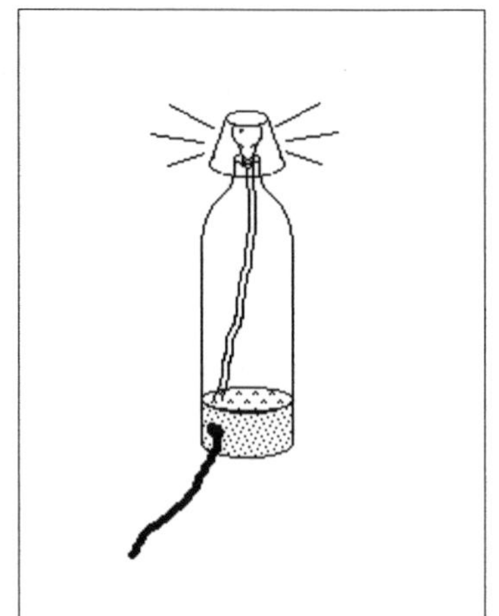

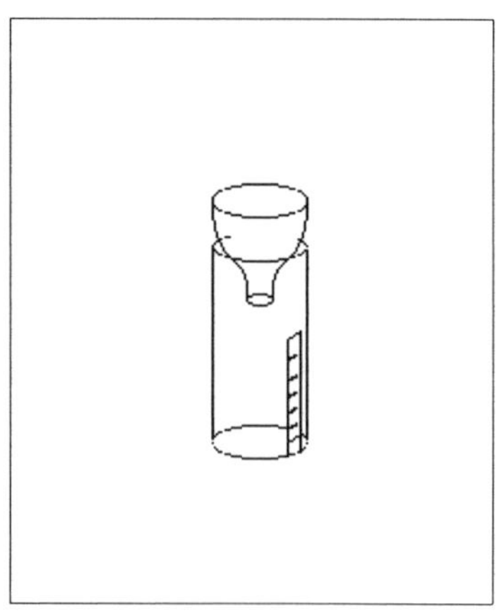

A plastic detergent bottle becomes a lighthouse in one context (top) and a rain gauge in another (directly above).

Essential Technical Supplies

Most of the materials needed for science activities are not highly technical, but schools will need to purchase some specialized equipment, since substitutes are either hard to find or awkward to use. For example, one or two powerful permanent magnets are essential to supplement the varied smaller magnets children will collect. There are no substitutes, either, for a few large hand magnifiers. Again, children will collect smaller ones for themselves, and these will suffice for some projects, but for others, satisfactory results can be obtained only with the real thing. The aim should always be to select materials that minimize difficulties and keep the essentials of a problem clearly before the children. Other specialized equipment that teachers will need to purchase is listed in Appendix B.

Most of the materials listed in Appendix B have been selected with an eye to their suitability for independent use by children. However, teachers will inevitably be called upon to assist with manipulative tasks or to help carry out children's overambitious construction plans. It is therefore helpful to keep a few simple tools on hand and to become proficient at using them. A very firm table or small workbench can make construction tasks much easier for the teacher. A few basic tools for the teacher's use are listed in the sidebar on the next page.

Sometimes teachers can help children considerably with manipulative problems by preparing certain technical items in advance. By preparing ready-made electrical connection leads, for example (crocodile clips at the ends of wires make excellent connectors), the difficulties children have in attaching wires to contacts will be minimized.

Computers and Software

The wide application of computers in today's world has led many educators to wonder whether children can and should be working with computers at an early age. Our own experiences in helping educators provide computer learning experiences for young children have convinced us that computers and good software are valuable, though optional, learning materials for children in kindergarten and the early primary grades. Computers and software can supplement the hands-on science materials that are used in the activities presented in Part 2 of this book.

When chosen carefully, computer materials can be a source of challenging, interactive activities that illuminate basic science concepts. In contrast to science worksheets that require children to produce "right answers," high quality, developmentally appropriate computer activities invite exploration and the generation of multiple solutions. For example, the program *Mystery Objects* (MECC) enables children to investigate the attributes of objects, while *Wood Car Ralley* (also from MECC) engages children in problem solving as they seek the best combination of features for small racing cars. Some other examples of good programs are the *Explore-a-Science* programs from D. C. Heath: *Animal Tracks, Wolves*, and *Whales*. The programs in this series allow children to create stories and colorful illustrations as they explore animal habitats. Still other computer programs allow children to explore physical phenomena or mechanisms, such as reflections, liquid mixtures, or gears. The key to successful computer activities is the selection of appropriate programs.

This chapter's guidelines for managing science activities within the daily schedule and for arranging the learning environment, taken together with the developmental teaching principles presented in Chapters 1, 2, and 3, constitute the basic elements of the High/Scope approach to teaching science. For a detailed listing of suggested science materials, again, consult Appendix B. Next, in Chapter 5, we present narrative examples of actual science activities that teachers have conducted using the child development principles, teaching strategies, and classroom management guidelines described in Chapters 1–4.

Simple Tools for the Teacher's Use

- Hammer (No. 0 or 1, not a heavy claw hammer)
- Bradawl (Size A, 1¼-in., for piercing holes before putting in screws
- "C" clamp, (4-in. or vise)
- Small screwdriver (electrician's)
- Medium screwdrivers (4-in. and 6-in.)
- Universal pliers (5-in. and needle nose)
- Hacksaw (one that cuts plastic or metal)
- Tenon saw (8-in., for cutting wood)
- Wire cutter
- Wire stripper (bib-stripper-type)
- Hand drill with ⅛-in., 3⁄16-in., and ¼-in. bits
- Triangular file (6-in.)
- Surform shaping tool (cuts wood, plastic, etc., like a file)
- Strong scissors

5

Case Histories of Effective Teaching

In previous chapters, we discussed the assumptions about child development that underlie our approach to science learning and the teaching and classroom management strategies needed to implement this approach. We now conclude this discussion with case histories of successful science activities. The following are all authentic examples taken from teachers' notes and accounts of their work. From reading these examples, we hope you'll gain an appreciation of the joys and complexities of using a developmental approach to science teaching. There is no recipe for this kind of teaching; it depends on the teacher's sensitivity, initiative, creativity, and ability to respond to the needs of the moment. The teaching framework we've presented is only a set of tools. It is up to individual teachers and the children in their classrooms to decide how to use these tools. Following the case histories, Part 2 of this book presents suggested science activities organized by the three broad themes introduced in Chapter 2: Life and Environment, Structure and Form, Energy and Change.

Looking at Leaves

Theme: Life and environment
Investigation: Leaf structures
Level: Kindergarten

The Setting

The setting was an early childhood school for children aged 5 to 8 years. The school served a suburban town recently developed in a previously rural area. The school site contained many trees, including horse chestnuts, oaks, beeches, and sweet chestnuts, as well as various small bushes, e.g., hawthorn, blackthorn, and privet. The classrooms were large, well-stocked, and organized for active learning. The immediate school site was the location for the walk.

Materials Provided

The teacher distributed plastic bags for collecting leaves. Once back in the classroom, she provided paper, paints, crayons, and glue and other materials for making leaf prints and mounting the leaves. Lengths of string were available to be used as measuring units.

General Experience the Teacher Had in Mind

■ For children to examine more closely a random collection of autumn leaves and to sort the collection according to several criteria on returning to the classroom.

Processes the Teacher Hoped to Encourage

■ For children to choose criteria for sorting, e.g., all the dark brown leaves, all the leaves with pointed shapes, all the leaves shaped like hands.

■ For children to record their experiences in different ways, e.g., leaf collections mounted on large sheets of paper, leaf outlines made by drawing around the edges of leaves, leaf prints, leaf rubbings, splatter prints.

■ For children to measure leaves and record the results, including measurements of surface area made by tracing leaves on squared paper.

Activities/Problem-Solving Situations the Teacher Hoped to Encourage

■ Making random collections of leaves on an autumn walk in the school grounds. Children would work in pairs, sharing the collecting, carrying, and conversation. Leaves could be gathered in plastic bags.

■ Noting which trees had lost most of their leaves either by observing the bareness of the tree or the piles of leaves near them.

■ Feeling the veins in the leaves and following their patterns.

■ Throwing leaves in the air and seeing which "flew" best.

■ Collecting leaves with unusual markings, colors, scars, and damage.

■ Using leaves as construction materials, e.g., making houses, huts, or tents out of leaves.

Activities That Actually Resulted

■ A "leaf walk" was organized on the school grounds. As expected, children collected leaves and filled their bags enthusiastically. Most of the collecting was random.

■ There was immense interest in the teacher's suggestion that they explore which leaves "flew" best. This stimulated much haphazard experimentation. The teacher intervened to suggest a way of making comparisons more systematic: using a common starting line for the flying races. The winning leaves were kept for further testing in the playground later on.

■ In the classroom the teacher encouraged children to examine the leaves more closely. Many children noticed several different kinds of marks on the leaves. With the teacher's help, children were able to identify particular marks as having been caused by leaf miners, physical damage (breakage or tearing), or decay. A group of children sorted their leaves according to the marks they found on them.

■ The children subjected the largest and smallest leaves to close measurement, with the teacher intervening to help formulate rules for deciding which leaves were big or small enough to be singled out for more exact measurement. The children used lengths of string as their measurement unit.

■ In spite of the teacher's hopes, no children chose to sort leaves by color. However, children were interested in sorting by shape. This provided a basis for helping children identify oak, horse chestnut, and beech leaves. Children also showed interest in ranking the leaves in each shape group from smallest to largest. The teacher helped children mount and label the resulting collections.

■ Leaf printing was a popular activity. The teacher helped children print using two techniques: splatter printing and printing by brushing paint on the leaves and pressing them down on paper.

■ Prints made from the largest and smallest leaves were mounted beside the original leaf collections.

■ Children also enjoyed experimenting with floating the leaves on water. Children tested the buoyancy of leaves of different sizes and shapes by loading them with paper clips one at a time and observing how many clips were needed to sink a leaf. The results were reported orally at review time.

■ Some children made leaf rubbings with crayons and tracing paper, thus revealing venation patterns.

■ No one was interested in using leaves as model-building materials!

Testing "Floaters" and "Sinkers"

Theme: Structure and form
Investigation: Testing and measuring properties
Level: First grade

The Setting

The school in which these activities took place was located in an industrial area in a large city. A great variety of scrap materials were readily available. The population of the area was multiracial, and the school reflected this ethnic mix.

Materials Provided

The teacher placed pieces of the following materials in the water table area: wood, cardboard, thick wallboard, Styrofoam, sheet metal, plastic, rubber, clay tiles. The materials were cut to the same approximate shape, size, and thickness as the 4-in.-square tiles. The teacher also provided nails and marbles, to be used as weights, and plastic lids to hold the weights.

General Experience the Teacher Had in Mind

■ For children to explore floating and sinking with some precision.

Processes/Activities/Problem-Solving Situations the Teacher Hoped to Encourage

■ For children to go beyond the random floating and sinking tests they usually tried and begin to explore floating and sinking with objects of like sizes.

■ For children to move beyond merely categorizing objects as "floaters" or "sinkers" and begin to compare the buoyancy of different materials by considering what load an object made from a particular material would support before sinking.

■ For children to consider the need for care and restraint in testing the materials.

■ For children to observe how absorbing water affects the buoyancy of some substances, e.g., cardboard and wallboard.

■ For interested children to test whether drying out a material improved its buoyancy.

Activities That Actually Resulted

■ The children immediately began working with the materials that the teacher introduced and began sorting out the "sinkers" and "floaters" as they had done in previous activities.

■ The teacher suggested children try using marbles as loads for their "rafts." However, children dismissed this as impossible, since they realized the marbles would roll off the rafts. The teacher then asked whether the plastic lids might be a help, and the children immediately saw that the lids could be used to hold the loads.

■ An unsystematic testing of rafts followed, with the group working in a random way. Children were mainly interested only in which person could load the most on a raft. The teacher's hopes for a neat set of results were completely thwarted.

■ After a while, the cardboard and the thick wallboard lost much of their buoyancy and this caught the children's interest. The children tried holding cardboard rafts under water and then tested them with the same loads as used before the soaking.

■ The children held Styrofoam rafts under water and tested them as they had done with the cardboard rafts, with very different results. The Styrofoam retained its buoyancy very well after soaking. The children also tried weighing down some Styrofoam rafts with tiles to keep them immersed longer, then tested them again. As the result of these tests, the children judged Styrofoam to be a "wonder floater."

■ While the teacher had hoped for a tidy set of results that could be posted on a chart, the children were not interested in this form of communication. They preferred simply talking about their experiences. Wisely, the teacher encouraged this.

■ Several days later some children illustrated an account of the "wonder floater" by gluing the actual materials on a drawing. At review time, the children reenacted the procedures they had used and again discussed the floating and sinking activity.

Comment

By accepting the forms of reporting that the children preferred, the teacher encouraged the children's continued enthusiasm and interest. Thus, when the subject arose again a few days later, she used this as an occasion for encouraging further reflection and dialogue about what had happened. Making a numerical chart is often a more attractive idea to teachers than to young children, unless their interest in a subject is especially high.

Experimenting With Wheels

Theme: Energy and change
Investigation: Simple machines
Level: Second grade

The Setting

These activities were carried out in a large urban school, housed in modern buildings on a large site. The teacher had the materials arranged in boxes, so that children could get out what they needed independently.

Materials Provided

The teacher made the following materials available: house bricks (varnished to seal them), thin rope, spring balances, string, thread spools of various sizes, nails of various lengths, rubber bands, pieces of wood to be used as bases for the carts, cardboard boxes of all sizes and strengths, wooden boxes and tins of various shapes and sizes, circular boxes; a collection of old wheel and wind-up toys, clocks, and wheels of all kinds; simple tools: hammers, pliers, hacksaws, screwdrivers, clamps, a workbench, and a vise.

General Experience the Teacher Had in Mind

■ For children to examine wheels as simple machines and provide firsthand experience with them in existing and child-invented devices.

Processes the Teacher Hoped to Encourage

■ For children to experience firsthand that rolling a load is easier than sliding it.

■ For children to observe that wheels make rolling possible and thus make it easier to move an object.

■ For children to observe and explore how some wheels turn other wheels in machines.

■ For children to explore the special relationships that exist when small wheels turn large wheels and vice versa.

■ For children to observe that the pulley is another use for wheels.

Activities/Problem-Solving Situations the Teacher Hoped to Encourage

■ Pulling a load by sliding it on the ground, then putting the same load on a skateboard and pulling it. Children could first make their comparisons intuitively, based on which load was easiest to pull, and then use a spring balance inserted in the pulling cord to make comparative measurements of the force needed to pull each load.

■ Describing and tabulating the results of these measurements.

■ Using everyday items, such as thread spools, nails, and small wooden boxes, to make simple carts for transporting loads.

■ Comparing the ease of pulling a load in the same small box with and without wheels. (A spring balance could be used to measure the force needed as in the preceding activity, but a finer calibration would be needed for this smaller-scale experiment.)

■ Exploring how wheels can be made to turn each other.

■ Observing the direction of turning when wheels turn each other.

■ Exploring how wheels are used in toys.

■ Noticing the special shapes of wheels used in wind-up toys.

■ Noticing how the pulley on the flagpole makes it easy to put up the flag.

Activities That Actually Resulted

■ Working in small groups, children set up both large- and small-scale experiments to investigate the use of wheels to compare sliding motion with rolling motion. In the large-scale experiment, children loaded a box with four house bricks and pulled it with a rope. Various children in the group tested the pull needed to move it. They then put the loaded box on a skateboard (with rope attached) and tested the pull needed to move the box.

■ The teacher intervened to suggest and demonstrate how to insert a spring scale into the pulling rope. The group repeated the experiment, this time using the scale to measure the force needed to pull the box with and without the skateboard.

■ Children made charts to illustrate the activity and report the results.

■ As two small groups worked with the bricks and large boxes, other small groups tested smaller loads in cigar-box carts and toy trucks. A sloping plank was used to test uphill pulls (see illustration).

■ The teacher intervened, as with the other group, to supply the know-how and the necessary spring scale for measuring the pulls. Children recorded the results pictorially after much group discussion on the best means to show what had been done.

■ Another group investigated the problem: Can wheels turn wheels? The teacher had supplied them with spools of various sizes, nails to use as spindles, and wood pieces suitable for mounting the spools. The children "invented" various solutions to this problem, including "friction drives," in which wheels turned each other by touching, and "rubber band drives," in which the wheels were connected by rubber bands. Some of their devices had large wheels driving small wheels; others had the reverse. The children were satisfied just to have achieved the transmission of motion. However, the teacher intervened to suggest a study of the following:

1. What happens to the direction of motion when one wheel drives another?

2. When a big wheel drives a small wheel, how does this affect the turning speed of the little wheel?

3. When a small wheel drives a large wheel, how does this affect the turning speed of the large wheel?

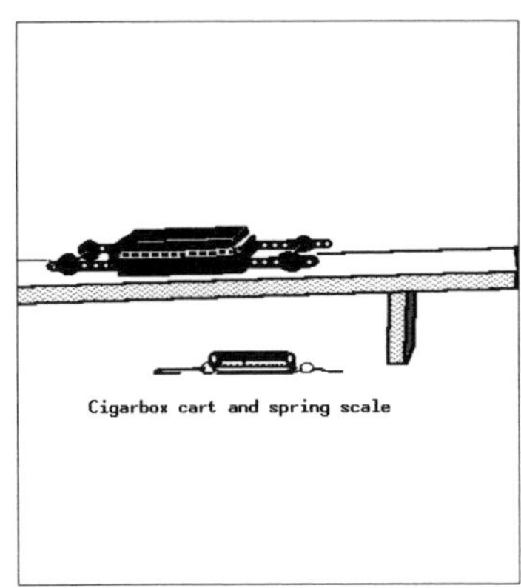

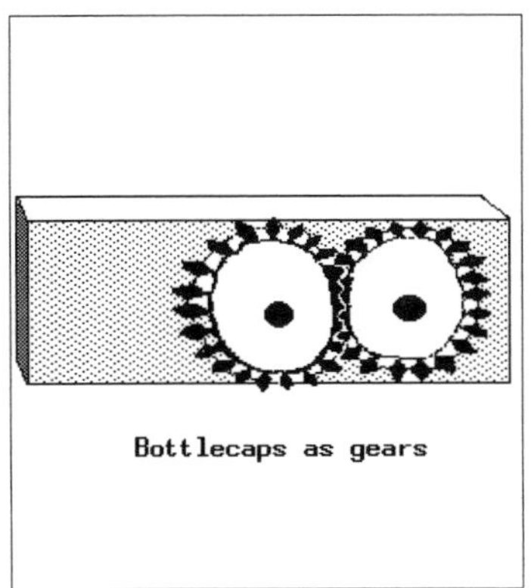

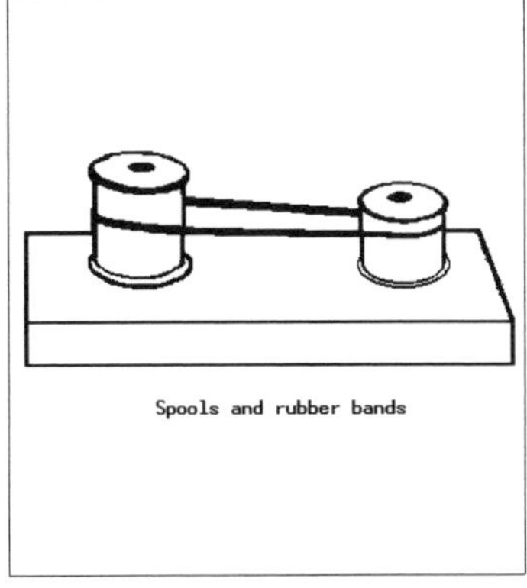

Some of the apparatus children built as they explored wheels are shown here. Children measured the force needed to pull a rolling load uphill using a cigar-box cart and spring scale (first illustration). They also explored the transmission of motion (center illustration), building a "friction drive" that used bottlecaps as gears and (bottom illustration) constructing a "rubber band drive" with spools as gears.

4. In a band drive, what happens to the motion of the wheels when the bands are crisscrossed in the middle rather than looped straight around the wheels?

■ Since time ran out, the activities were carried over to the next day. The next day's session began with a lively discussion of the various day's experiments, with much discussion of how results might be recorded. The teacher had intended to steer the class to the problems of how pulleys work, but the class was more intent on an animated discussion of the activities they had already done. So she passed out a large selection of simple mechanisms from the collections she had made—toy cars, old clocks, rotary egg beaters, model trains, and so forth—and asked each group to use its new knowledge of wheels to look critically at these simple machines. Then she asked the children to report their conclusions to the whole class. This resulted in a much more productive session than the discussion of the pulley on a flagpole! The standard of reporting and communicating was very high, with the children making intelligent guesses when they were unable to reason something out.

Comment

The teacher in this activity acted as an enabler, encourager, leader, and supplier of materials. She used good judgment about when to interject her own suggestions, questions, and priorities, so that the flow of the children's activities was not interrupted. The result was good science education.

Working With Bridges

Theme: Structure and form
Investigation: Stability of structures
Level: Third grade

The Setting

The school was located in a country market town through which a small river flows. In addition to several river bridges, there were also road and railway bridges in the area. Thus there were many local examples of bridges that the children could study firsthand.

Materials Provided

The teacher provided the following materials for the building activities: ample supplies of typing paper and newspaper, sheets of thin poster board (postcard weight), ½-in. cellophane tape, glue, large supply of 1-in. nails to use as loads, matchboxes, straws, four sets of weights (¼-, ½-, 1-, 2-, and 7-lb), scissors, and rulers. The teacher deliberately limited the materials supplied to those on this list to encourage innovation and to help to keep the structures uniform enough to be comparable.

General Experiences the Teacher Had in Mind

■ For children to think about the problem of bridging a gap.

■ For children to test some common bridge designs and, in so doing, to test the strength of different structural shapes.

Processes the Teacher Hoped to Encourage

■ For children to explore ways to measure the strengths of structures by simple standardized means, so results could be compared.

■ For children to test the strength of model bridges built to different designs and with different materials.

■ For children to design bridges to meet specific criteria, e.g., to carry very light loads, to carry heavy loads, to bridge wide spaces using two middle supports, or to bridge wide spaces using no middle supports.

■ For children to survey the area around the school and document all the bridging methods that could be observed.

Activities/Problem-Solving Situations the Teacher Hoped to Encourage

■ Making a collection of pictures of bridges in the locality, by photographing them, drawing them, or making clippings from newspapers or magazines, and then noticing and exploring the different designs found. Some of the following questions could arise as children looked at a

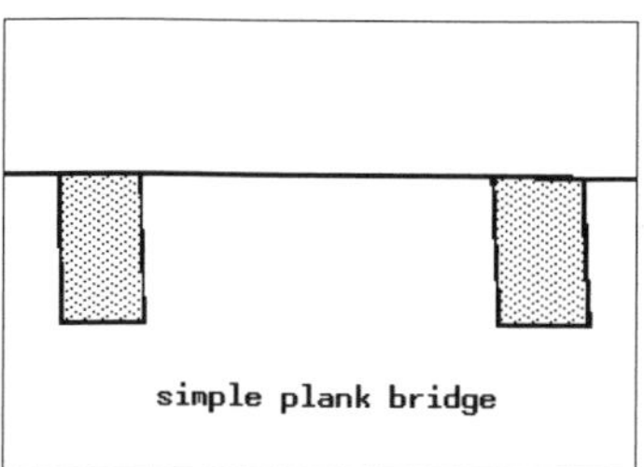

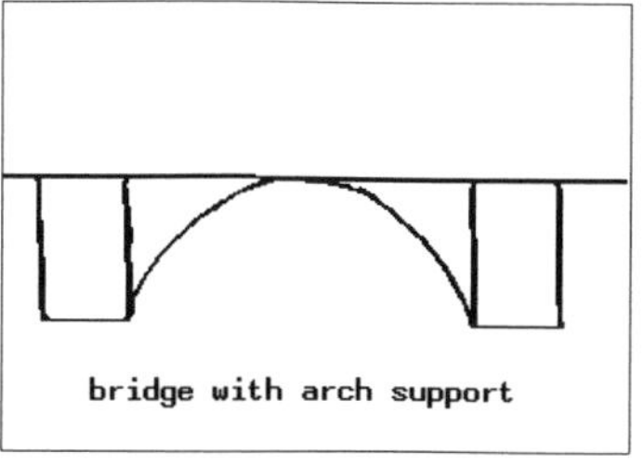

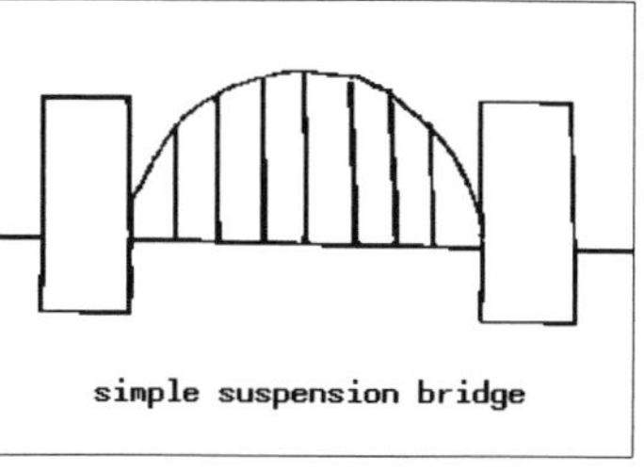

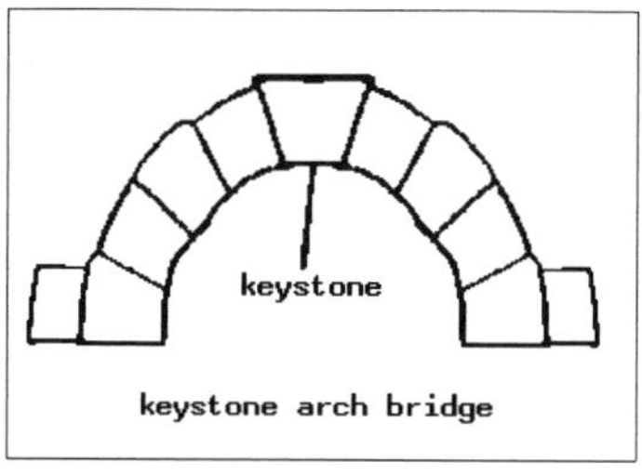

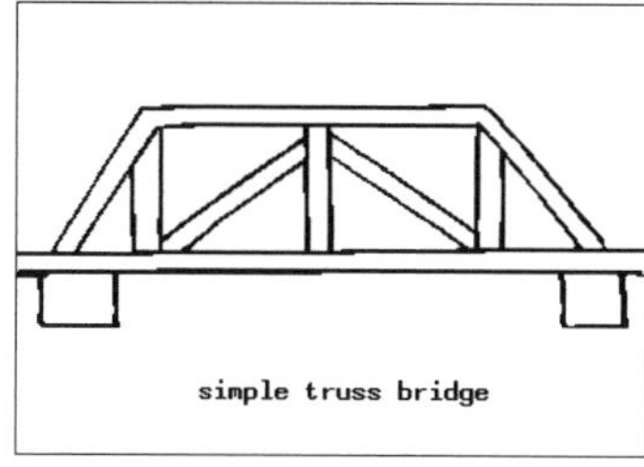

Here are some of the basic bridge designs children explored.

particular bridge: How is the bridge made? How wide is the gap to be bridged? What materials are used? What is the general structure of the bridge? How heavy is traffic on the bridge? How old is the bridge?

■ With the simple materials provided, making bridges of different designs and testing their strength with nails, weights, or both. The teacher planned to suggest that children make several basic bridge designs (see sidebar), to bridge a 6-in. gap between two piles of books, using 3-inch-wide strips of poster paper and the other materials listed previously.

■ After each basic structure had been built and tested, exploring what these results indicated concerning the strengths of flat and cylindrical bridge beams.

■ Making and testing other, more complex bridge shapes (e.g., a suspension bridge) using the materials given. The teacher planned to encourage children to try using newspaper to build a bridge over an 18-in. gap to support the weight of two children. Another possible activity she planned was to encourage children to explore whether an arch could be built and tested for strength with the available materials.

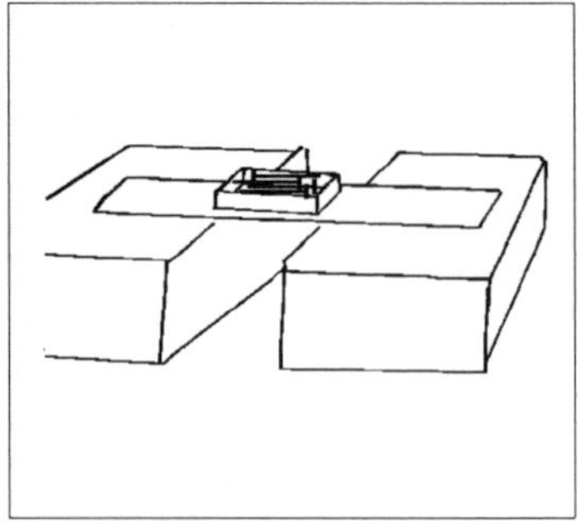

A single plank bridge constructed of one strip of poster board was the simplest bridge design built and tested by the children.

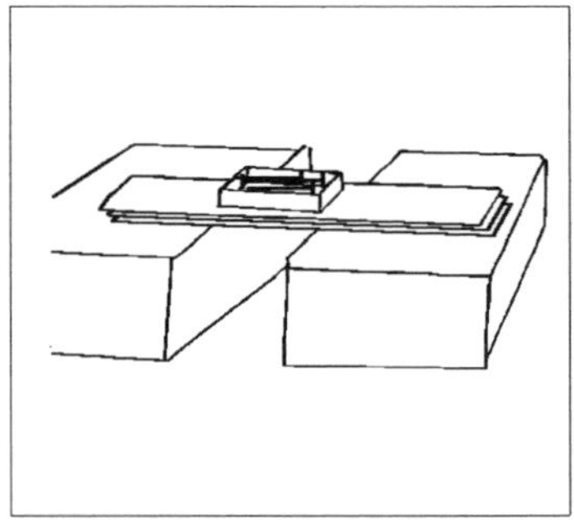

Children made another kind of single plank bridge by gluing three strips of poster paper together to form a thicker plank.

Activities That Actually Resulted

■ Children identified the general types of bridges in the area from the collection of photographs, drawings, and clippings they collected. They discussed the problems the bridge builders faced and the materials they used. They wrote captions for the pictures describing the bridge designs and construction materials.

■ Children carried out the "bridging the gap" activities, using the suggested gap of 6 in. between two piles of books. They used the nails and weights provided to test the strength of the bridge designs they created. The teacher encouraged them to standardize the designs, so testing would be more meaningful. The basic unit used was a single plank consisting of a 3-inch-wide strip of paper. Children tested the strengths of simple plank bridges made from one strip, then proceeded to build and test multi-plank bridges of up to eight strips stacked together. The multi-plank bridges were tested both with planks unfastened and with planks glued together.

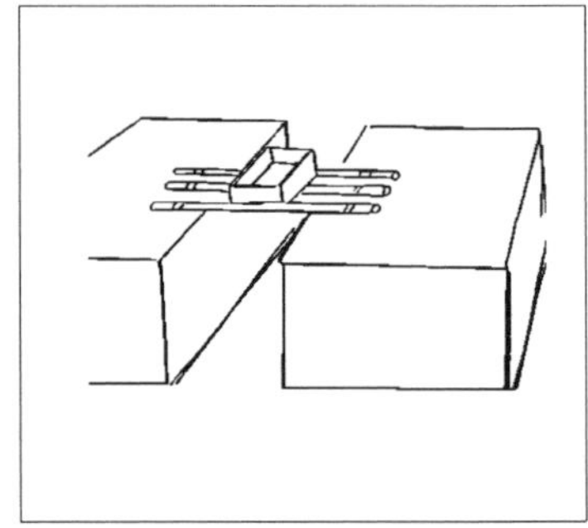

Children also constructed simple beam bridges, such as this one using three rolled strips of typing paper as the beams.

■ Bridge construction and testing was repeated using paper rolled into cylinders to construct beam bridges.

■ Other, more complex bridge designs were also invented and tested as planned, using only 3-in. strips and glue as the raw materials.

■ Children made a table of the results of these experiments and wrote out comments on the findings.

■ After discussing and considering their previous bridge-building experiences, the children followed the teacher's suggestion that they work at designing bridges for light loads, heavy loads, and very heavy loads.

■ The gap between the books was widened to 12 in., and the group considered how best to bridge this gap. Children then set about making a cantilever-type bridge with two central supports, a suspension bridge, and an arched bridge.

■ Using much newspaper and glue, children engaged in building a bridge over an 18-in. gap that would take the weight of any child in the class.

■ The teacher encouraged children to keep exact records of all the materials used, so the results of the different groups could be compared.

■ The bridge-building activities continued for over a month. The teacher encouraged children to work in small groups and pairs, working on aspects of the main topic that particularly interested them. At the end of a month, a grand exhibition of bridges and bridging techniques was presented. Bridge models built by children were displayed. Test results were presented in both chart and narrative form. Tape recordings were made available of interviews with the builders. In these tapes, the builders described, for example, the collapse of some bridges under testing and the conclusions drawn from the tests. Children also made displays of drawings and photographs of bridges in the locality that included some little-known footbridges in the nearby countryside.

▼
Part 2
Activities for K–3 Science

6

Introducing the Science Activities

This chapter introduces sample K–3 science activities that embrace the instructional principles, key experiences, and thematic outline discussed in the preceding chapters. As we prepare to introduce the science activities, it is essential that we look, for a moment, beyond them to the broader context of child and teacher roles in carrying out these activities. For a developmentally oriented approach to be effective, adults must monitor the quality both of their own initiatives (the activities and instruction they conduct) and of children's initiatives (their work with materials, their thinking, their ideas, and their questions). The science activities and background material presented in the chapters that follow this one are intended as starting points for activities in science. They provide a foundation for making science a vital part of daily classroom and personal life. The measure of their success will be the extent to which they infuse the classroom with science-related activity and enrich ongoing activity with science understanding.

Presentation of the Activities

Group Size

Most of the activities that follow are designed for small-group "workshop" sessions, though (as we note in italics in specific activities) a few are intended for large groups. As described in Chapter 4, the small-group workshop sessions we envision involve tasks, or activities, that are introduced by the teacher and then carried out with the teacher providing judicious support as small groups of children work quite independently. However, teachers may find that they can adapt any of the science activities either for a small or a large group. (See "Which Brand Is Best" at right for an example of how a large-group science activity might proceed.) They may even occasionally adapt an activity to a two-part format, i.e., a large-group introduction followed up with small-group or individual work. We encourage teachers to work with small groups whenever possible because of the greater degree of active involvement that can be achieved in such a setting.

Assembling appropriate materials for the science activities usually requires the most effort when small-group activities are planned, since each child or pair of children will need a set of materials, but the benefits of using small groups do justify the extra effort. Teachers will find it easier to follow through on their commitment to work with small groups if they gather materials well in advance, accumulate them over time, and enlist children and their parents in helping to collect and prepare materials.

Selection of Content

The science activities we present here do not exhaust or cover comprehensively our three broad themes—Life and Environment, Structure and Form, and Energy and Change. Rather, they merely suggest the nature of appropriate K–3 science activities within each of these themes. In selecting content, we have been guided by two overriding aims: first, to provide children with opportunities for the science key experiences and, second, to present science content involving causes and systems that children can apprehend directly, by using their senses and by exploring and manipulating objects and mechanisms. For

Which Brand Is Best? A Typical Science Activity

The following is a description of the flow of events in a typical science activity. The activity was planned around "Analyzing Mixtures," p. 118. Though the activity described here is conducted with an entire class, it could be adapted for a small-group workshop.

Earlier in the year, children in Ms. Tew's second-grade class carried out a number of science and math activities involving classification. They classified leaves and sorted seeds early in the fall when natural specimens were available. Wishing to extend the children's experience in this area, Ms. Tew has planned a science workshop around analyzing mixtures. She expects that children will use key experiences in classifying and analyzing as they carry out the activity.

To begin the activity, Ms. Tew shows the children three boxes of raisin bran, including two different standard brands and one generic variety. Her plan is to give a brief introduction to the process of analyzing, and then, with children working in pairs, to give them small samples of cereal to analyze on their own.

Spreading a sample of one of the cereals on a large piece of paper, and showing the children a small paper cup (3-ounce size), she asks the children to estimate how many raisins and flakes they might find in a cup of cereal. Several children make counts and estimates of raisins and flakes. "Is there anything else you might find this reason, our activities place a heavy emphasis on building projects in which children work with simple technologies, e.g., building with materials of all kinds, exploring objects with moving parts, or working with simple gadgets and machines. We emphasize these kinds of experiences because they allow children to grapple with the simple causal mechanisms that come to play when objects touch, bump, push, pull, and interlock with one another. As children build and explore objects and simple machines, for example, they can manipulate such factors as speed, force, timing, and distance and observe the effects. In contrast, the causal mechanisms that govern changes in living things and their ecosystems are, for the most part, far too complex for children in this age group to understand and manipulate directly. As a result, you will notice that activities under the Life and Environment theme tend to be largely descriptive, focusing on observing, classifying, identifying, and ordering. Though these descriptive activities are worthwhile, we encourage an emphasis on activities involving simple technologies because of the wider experience with causal mechanisms these afford.

Sequencing of Activities

Rather than using the science activities in the sequence we present them in, a teacher may use them in virtually any sequence that is consistent with the teacher's understanding of children's developmental levels. Several "logical" mini-sequences may be found within the activities, however (e.g., one sequence involving seed germination and growth and another concerning structures built with triangles). It may be desirable to preserve the order in these mini-sequences, since their activities usually relate to a central topic, sometimes build on one another, and often require similar equipment or supplies.

Grade-Level Indications

A suggested grade-level range is indicated at the top of each activity. We have designated a range rather than a single grade level because we recognize that age is often a poor predictor of children's development or interest. Also, the activities often include options (such as suggestions for more sophisticated measurement) that make them adaptable to more than one developmental or grade level. In addition, some of the suggestions for extension of an ac-

in the cereal?" Ms. Tew goes on.

She then asks the children how they might record their findings about the number of flakes and raisins. Several children suggest using a block graph in which the number of raisins or flakes corresponds to filled-in. squares on the graph paper (a technique children used in a recent math workshop). She then asks children to predict whether the number of raisins might differ from one brand to another. Several children make predictions, guessing that the brands their families usually buy will have the most raisins.

Ms. Tew asks the children to find partners. She then asks each pair to use small paper cups to sample each of two brands, separate out the parts of each mixture, compare the results, and then record their findings in some way. Plain paper, squared graph paper, pencils, and markers are available at each of the tables where children are working.

As children begin to work, Ms. Tew circulates among them to help them get started and ask what they are finding out about the mixtures: "I see that you've sorted your raisin bran into raisins and flakes, Todd. Were you surprised to find so many raisins? . . . How many did you find? . . . What about yours, Jeff? . . . How many raisins did you find? . . . Since you had the same brand as Todd, why do you think you didn't get the same results? . . . Why don't you both get another cup of the same brand and separate it to see if you get the same results?"

After about 10 minutes, most teams of children have analyzed their samples and tivity call for skills and abilities that may be considerably more advanced than those involved in the main activity.

Key Experiences

Each activity includes a listing called Key Experiences, which designates the key experience (or experiences) most central to the activity. The key experience designations will help teachers to view each activity within the overall scope and sequence of the science program. Of course, many other key experiences may arise during the course of an activity, and teachers should be alert for opportunities to build on these. Children will also have opportunities for many additional key experiences through the suggestions for extension of the science activities, and through "spin-off" projects and pursuits that children initiate during plan-do-review times.

Questions to Ask

Sample questions are included in a Questions to Ask section of each activity. These are not meant to be used in a scripted, word-for-word way; rather, teachers should use them as models in developing their own questions to help children elaborate their thoughts and focus on important ideas. As much as possible, the questions are composed in an open-ended style designed to elicit children's thinking and to lead them to further, independent exploration of the topic.

Related Reading

Brief lists of books and related materials are included in the Related Reading section of each activity. The lists include some sources written as children's books. These may be made available as background resources or used as text materials for whole-group or individual reading. Other reference materials are intended for adults seeking further information about the topic at hand. Many include useful illustrations that may be used to supplement the hands-on activity. Some of the references relate to the Extension suggestions for an activity and may be of particular interest for children and teachers planning to pursue related projects and activities of their own design.

have begun to construct graphs to show the results. Some have chosen to make object graphs, gluing the raisins and flakes one by one directly onto the squares of the graph paper. Others are making block graphs, coloring squares one by one to represent the quantities of raisins and flakes. Others are making charts on which they are gluing small groupings of raisins and flakes, labeled with the actual numbers they have counted.

Later, the children share their experiences and their charts and graphs with the whole group. Ms. Tew tabulates the raisin counts for all the samples on the blackboard, organizing them by brand. The children discuss the differences between the samples of raisin bran. Some of the children have added another category to their analyses—partial flakes or cereal dust that they found in their cups. Many of the children insist that a particular brand offers the most raisins. Several children, however, observe that even the generic raisin bran offers nearly as many raisins per cup as the standard brands. There is a discussion of the relative cost of the brands and the relationship between cost and the number of raisins.

To end the session, Ms. Tew shows the children several additional mixtures—more cereals, a bird seed mixture, and a package of mixed beans. She explains that these mixtures will be placed in the science center and suggests that children may wish to continue their analyzing during a plan-do-review period.

Later in the day, several children do indeed choose the science area for the plan-do-review activity. They set about analyzing the mixtures placed there. Tracia

Extension

To each activity are appended one or more Extension suggestions—activities that may be pursued in small- or large-group settings or in independent work. These "spin-off" activities vary considerably and may involve adapting or extending the original activity to a different developmental level, a different setting, a different but related topic, or a longer time-frame.

The extension suggestions given only begin to tap the many possibilities for relating science learning to other themes and content areas under study in the classroom. Because ours is a flexible approach that emphasizes broad processes rather than rigidly defined content, teachers usually see many opportunities for integrating science experiences with other curriculum areas or content themes that a group may be focusing on. For example, in nearly every activity, we encourage children to document their work in some form—a chart, model, display, or graph—and these provide natural contexts for children to apply math and language skills in meaningful ways. Science experiences are also easily integrated with social studies themes. For example, when children have had an experience working firsthand with a simple technology—e.g., building teepees—this often sparks their interest in relating this technology to the lifestyles and histories of different peoples. We have tried to include a few suggestions for these kinds of tie-ins in the extension sections of the activities. However, these suggestions are merely intended as "starters"; alert teachers will generate many more ideas of their own.

Developing Additional Activities

While the activities in the next three chapters should be sufficient to launch a vigorous and developmentally sound science program, we encourage teachers to develop additional activities that reflect their own and, above all, their students' interests and that take advantage of materials and resources available in particular sites. We have gone to some lengths to explain our active learning methods, our developmental framework, and our emphasis on science activity involving an understanding of systems and causality. Our purpose has been to equip the reader both

asks Ms. Tew if she can analyze some potting soil that was used in a planting activity several weeks earlier. Tracia has been puzzled by the white bits she saw in the mixture. After Tracia has separated and analyzed the mixture, Ms. Tew refers her to a book on houseplants that explains the components of potting soil and their function. ■

to make informed and selective use of existing science curriculum resources and to develop his or her own science activities.

The three basic principles that should be kept uppermost in mind in pursuing this goal are to make science learning active for the child, to work with key experiences in mind, and to focus on science activities in which systems and causality are accessible to the child. Applied diligently, this approach can lead to many valuable and exciting science learning experiences.

7

▼

Life and Environment

Grades K–2

Planting Seeds

Examining seeds and providing the conditions for them to germinate

Key Experiences

- Classifying materials into small groups based on common attributes
- Building simple containers or environments for living things
- Observing and describing a pattern of change

Materials

For each pair of children: a mixture of 10–12 kinds of purchased vegetable seeds (e.g., bean, cucumber, squash, tomato); some paper or plastic foam egg cartons (foam cartons must have small holes for drainage); potting soil; spoons or garden trowels; tape; a magic marker; and a watering can

Activity

Children first sort the seeds into piles of like seeds, examining them to notice the similarities and differences. Then they plant two or three like seeds in potting soil in each cup of an egg carton. (They can tape an "identifying seed" to the outside of each cup and write their own names on the carton, so they will remember which seeds are planted and who planted them.) Finally, they water and set the filled egg cartons aside, for about a week, in a sunny spot. The responsibility for watering the planted seeds over the week can be divided among the children.

Seeds and seedlings are plant material in a form that is easy for children to observe, care for, and test. As one part of the important cycle of plant growth and reproduction, sprouting seeds can introduce children to living systems, their composition, and their response to environmental factors.

Questions to Ask

How many different kinds of seeds did you find in your mixture of seeds? How are they different? Do any of them look like seeds you've seen before? What do you think will grow from them? What are some things seeds need to grow? How long do you think it will take the seeds to sprout? How many seeds did you plant?

Extension

Using wild plant and flower seeds collected from a field trip, children sort and plant these in potting soil.

Related Reading

Jennings, Terry. *Seeds and Seedlings.* Chicago: Children's Press, 1989.

Pringle, Laurence. *Being a Plant* (pp. 46–50). New York: Thomas Y. Crowell, 1983.

Sabin, Louis. *Plants, Seeds, and Flowers.* Mahwah, NJ: Troll Associates, 1985.

Shuttlesworth, Dorothy. *The Hidden Magic of Seeds* ("Seed Magic," pp. 6–9; "What Is Inside a Seed," pp. 10–13). Emmaus, PA: Rodale Press, 1976.

Grades 1–3

Seed Watching

Seeing what happens to a seed as it sprouts

Key Experiences

- Observing changes over time
- Reporting sequences of events

Materials

For each pair of children: several small plastic bags (the kind that zip closed); white blotting paper, felt, or paper towel to line the plastic bags; sawdust; quick-growing seeds (mung beans, for example)

Activity

After lining a plastic bag with the white absorbent material, children fill the bag interior with sawdust to hold the lining in place and to hold moisture. Then they put beans between the bag and its lining and add water to the bag until the lining is wet but not dripping. Finally they place the bags somewhere in the room where they can water them regularly and observe them over time. They can record what they see in drawings, by tape-recorded comment, or by charts.

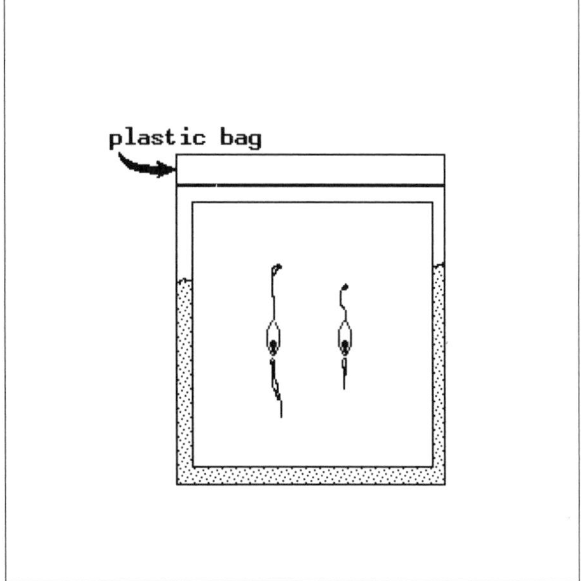

Questions to Ask

How many beans germinated in each bag? Did some sprout earlier than others? Are there any reasons you can think of for this? Is there a pattern to the growth? When did you first see a root developing? When did you see root hairs? Which way does the root push? Which way does the shoot push? How will you record all this?

Extension

1. Children explore using different planting media for some fast-growing seeds—damp sand, damp sawdust, damp styrofoam, damp thick cardboard—and plant 10 seeds in each. Then they observe which seeds grow fastest or best. Devising and discussing ways to assess and compare growth (e.g., counting the number of sprouts,

measuring the sprouts) and then graphing the results are good applications for children's developing math skills.

2. Children plant some slow-growing seeds such as broad beans and peas (after soaking them for 24 hours) and note how long they take to germinate, compared to the quick-growing seeds.

3. Again using the plastic bags for observation of germination, children try planting a broad bean in different orientations (with its scar, or *hilum*, downward, to the right, upward). They also plant half a bean with a scar, and without a scar. They then discover what effect this has on sprouting.

Related Reading

Jennings. Terry. *Seeds and Seedlings*. Chicago: Children's Press, 1989.

Rahn, Joan Elma. *Watch It Grow, Watch It Change* (pp. 75–82). New York: Atheneum, 1978.

Selsam, Millicent. *Play With Plants* (pp. 55–58). New York: William Morrow & Co., 1978.

Shuttlesworth, Dorothy. *The Hidden Magic of Seeds* (pp. 36–39). Emmaus, PA: Rodale Press, 1976.

Grades K–2

Observing Seedlings

Measuring growth changes in plant seedlings

Key Experiences

- Measuring properties and changes using standard or nonstandard whole units
- Measuring by producing a length to match another length
- Reporting sequences of events

Materials

For each pair of children: egg cartons with germinated seeds (from earlier activity); paper strips, scissors, and markers for recording heights (or rulers, for children who are able to use standard units)

Activity

Using the germinated seeds they planted previously in egg cartons, children observe and record the growth progress of the seedlings. If they are not ready to use standard units of measurement, they can cut strips of paper to match the heights of the seedlings at one-week intervals and paste these on a piece of paper to form a graph of each seedling's progress.

Questions to Ask

Did all the seeds you planted sprout? Which germinated best? How are the seedlings changing? How have you measured their growth? Are some seedlings changing faster than others? What reasons can you think of for this? How will you record your findings?

Extension

Children transfer some of the seedlings, when they are mature enough, to an outdoor vegetable garden. (Keeping the garden small, following the directions for planting on the various seed packets, and watering and cultivating the garden regularly are all important for a successful school garden.) Children keep a garden "diary," an activity that encourages them to observe changes over time. (This activity can also provide an excellent opportunity for practicing writing skills in a meaningful context, and can be a good vehicle for teachers to document the development of children's writing skills over time.) By harvesting some of the crops but also letting some go to seed, the children experience the entire growth cycle.

Related Reading

Jennings. Terry. *Seeds and Seedlings*. Chicago: Children's Press, 1989.

Rahn, Joan Elma. *Watch It Grow, Watch It Change* (pp. 75–82). New York: Atheneum, 1978.

Selsam, Millicent. *Play With Plants*, (pp. 55–58). New York: William Morrow & Co., 1978.

Shuttlesworth, Dorothy. *The Hidden Magic of Seeds*, (pp. 36–39). Emmaus, PA: Rodale Press, 1976.

Grades 1–2

Seed Sources

Discovering everyday sources of seeds and realizing that these seeds propagate plants

Key Experiences

- Taking something apart to observe it more closely
- Observing and describing a pattern of change

Materials

Apples, oranges (with seeds), watermelon, winter or hard squash, cherry tomatoes, wheat stalks, dried flowers—enough so that each child can choose a seed source; a dehydrator or an oven; potting soil and a container for each child to plant his/her seeds

Activity

Children separate seeds from various mature fruits, grains, or flowers, and then learn how they can clean and dry them to prepare them for planting. After drying the seeds in a dehydrator or a very slow oven (1–2 hours), they plant them in potting soil, moisten, and watch for signs of growth. Each container can be labeled with the seed source and with the name of the child who planted the seeds.

While it is easy for adults to realize that corn kernels they eat from the cob are the same as the corn seeds used to plant corn, many children, and even adolescents, do not connect the two. This activity can help children to realize that all seeds at one time were part of a growing plant and that the seeds found in common fruits, vegetables, grains, and flowers are indeed able to produce growing plants.

Questions to Ask

What are some ways the various seeds are different? What are some ways they are alike? What kinds of seeds did you choose to dry and plant? What do you think will grow from the seeds you plant? When there are no people around to plant seeds, how do new plants get started?

Extension

Since seeds of wheat and annual rye grass can be grown to maturity over three to four months, children plant these seeds and see them grow to maturity and produce new seeds for planting, all within the school year.

Related Reading

Foster, Willine K., & Quere, Pearl. *Seeds Are Wonderful.* Chicago: Melmont Publishers, 1960.

Prime, C. T., & Klein, Aaron E. *Seedlings and Soil* ("Seed Germination and Seedlings," pp. 23–38). Garden City, NY: Doubleday & Co., Inc., 1973.

Rahn, Joan Elma. *Grocery Store Botany* (pp. 33–48). New York: Atheneum, 1974.

Selsam, Millicent. *Play With Plants* (pp. 47–55). New York: William Morrow & Co., 1978.

Selsam, Millicent. *The Tomato and Other Fruit Vegetables.* New York: William Morrow & Co., 1970.

Shuttlesworth, Dorothy. *The Hidden Magic of Seeds* (pp. 26–35). Emmaus, PA: Rodale Press, 1976.

Grades 1–2

Sprouts for Eating

Experiencing how plant material may be more edible in one form than another

Key Experiences

- Observing change over time
- Observing the quantity of a material
- Observing and describing a pattern of change

Materials

For each pair of children: a tray from a commercial sprouter or a shallow pan with moist paper toweling; mung beans or alfalfa seeds for sprouting; crackers and cheese, or salad ingredients

Activity

Children place seeds in a sprouter and then water and set them aside for sprouting. When sprouts are ready (in two or three days), they try adding them to small cracker-and-cheese sandwiches or to salad, for a snack.

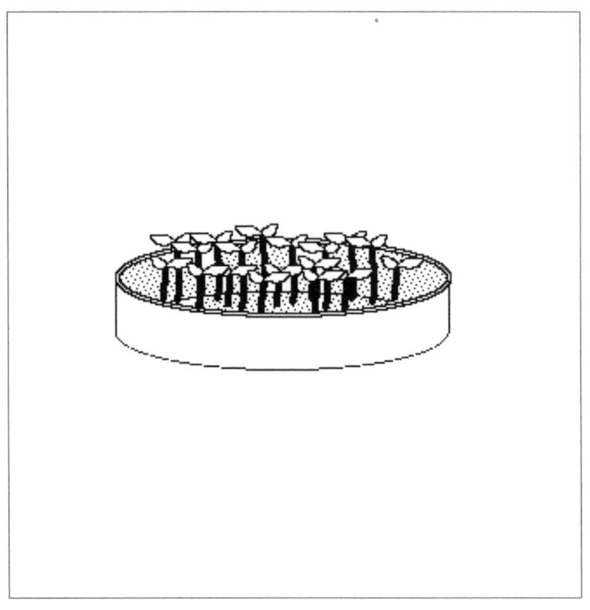

In the case of alfalfa seeds and mung beans, sprouting—by transforming the hard seeds into soft and moist young plants—makes this food source easier to eat. Besides observing this difference in usefulness, children can also observe the difference in quantity—how a small amount of seed produces a large bulk of edible matter.

Extension

1. To further illustrate the food potential of seeds, children use sprouts as a food source for a classroom pet, such as a gerbil, hamster, or rabbit.

2. Children carefully weigh a batch of seeds that are to be sprouted (on a small balance or spring scale—a letter scale may work well for this). After adding moisture to the seeds to make them sprout and then extracting the moisture by drying the sprouts in a dehydrator, the children weigh the sprouts. Despite the loss of water content, the weight of the dried plant material (sprouts) will be greater than the weight of the original plant material (seeds). Dis-

cussing where this weight might have come from introduces children to the fact that plants manufacture solid material out of air and water alone!

Related Reading

Johnsen, Jan. *Gardening Without Soil* ("Sprouting Seeds," pp. 7–10). New York: Lippincott, 1979.

Rahn, Joan Elma. *Watch It Grow, Watch It Change* (pp. 70–73, 75–77). New York: Atheneum, 1978.

Shuttlesworth, Dorothy E. *The Hidden Magic of Seeds* (pp. 30–34, 36–38). Emmaus, PA: Rodale Press, 1976.

Weiner, Michael A. *Man's Useful Plants* (pp. 22–25). New York: Macmillan Publishing Co., 1976.

Grades K–1

Popcorn: An "Exploded" Seed

Discovering popping as another way of converting a seed to edible form

Key Experiences

- Observing and describing a pattern of change
- Manipulating physical objects to produce an effect or change

Materials

Popcorn on the cob (available at farm markets or specialty stores); a popcorn popper; oil (if the popper requires it); paper bowls or cups; salt; napkins

Activity

(Suitable for a large group)

Children shell kernels of popcorn from cobs, then collect the kernels and pop them in a popper. Then they compare the size, weight, appearance, and edibility of the popcorn before and after popping.

Popcorn is familiar to most children, but its connection with growing plants may not be. By starting with popcorn in its natural state—on the cob—children can begin to see this connection. Since corn is one of the foods that European settlers adopted from native peoples in the new world, this activity might be integrated with a unit on Indian culture and history in the Americas. This activity is suggested for a large group, so there can be adult supervision of the corn popping.

Questions to Ask

What was the popcorn like before it was popped? How did it change when it was popped? Which would you rather eat? Why? Where do you think the cobs of popcorn come from? What do you think would happen if we planted a kernel of popcorn that has not been popped? That has been popped?

Extension

1. Children make a simple graph comparing the size of popcorn seeds before and after popping. For example, they line up a column of 10 unpopped kernels beside a

column of 10 popped kernels, gluing them to a lightweight card.

2. Children plant some unpopped kernels in potting soil and watch them sprout, verifying that they are indeed seeds capable of producing new corn plants.

Related Reading

Fenton, Carroll Lane, & Kitchen, Herminie B. *Plants That Feed Us* (pp. 11–15). New York: The John Day Co., 1956.

McGrath, Susan. *Fun With Physics.* Washington, DC: National Geographic Society, 1986. (Pictures of popcorn popping and other photos)

Wyler, Rose. *Science Fun With Peanuts and Popcorn.* Morristown,NJ: Messner, 1985.

Grades 2–3

Flour—Food From Seeds

Discovering grinding as another way to convert seeds to edible form

Key Experiences

- Looking at familiar things in a new way
- Manipulating physical objects to produce an effect or change
- Observing and describing a pattern of change

Materials

For each pair of children: a mortar and pestle or a pair of flat stones, for grinding seeds; dried kernels of wheat and corn (available from a natural food or farm supply store); a flour sifter ; purchased whole wheat flour and corn meal

Activity

Children grind the wheat and corn seeds into flour (or meal) and then compare the results with the store-bought flour and meal. Then they sift the flour and meal they ground to arrive at a product they can use for baking.

Seeds are important sources of very concentrated nutrients that we need for life. Here children learn that the flour used in breads, cookies, and cakes comes from seeds of plants—wheat and corn, for example—and that grinding those seeds makes them useable for baking.

Questions to Ask

How did the kernels of wheat (corn) change when they were ground? What happened when the ground wheat (corn) was sifted? Could you bake something with the product you got after sifting? Could you bake cookies with the kernels of wheat (corn) before they were ground and sifted? Why do you think wheat is ground into flour? If you chew a wheat kernel, how does it taste? How does the taste compare to the taste of whole wheat flour?

Extension

1. Using the wheat (or corn) product they have produced—and some additional flour or meal (which the

teacher makes by grinding a larger quantity of kernels in a blender)—children bake cookies or muffins.

2. Children read about and draw the parts of a wheat kernel—the husk, the bran (or "coat"), the endosperm, and the germ—and learn what happens to these parts in the modern milling process.

3. Children visit a flour mill, a natural foods bakery, a cereal factory, a pasta factory, to see how wheat is processed or used in food products

Related Reading

Fenton, Carroll Lane, & Kitchen, Herminie B. *Plants That Feed Us* (pp. 11–15, 17–20). New York: The John Day Co., 1956.

Patent, Dorothy Hinshaw. *Wheat: The Golden Harvest.* New York: Putnam Publishing Group, 1987.

Rahn, Joan Elma. *Grocery Store Botany* (pp. 37–38). New York: Atheneum, 1974.

Weiner, Michael A. *Man's Useful Plants* (pp. 30–32). New York: Macmillan Publishing Co., 1976.

Grades 2–3

Oils—Food From Seeds

Discovering that vegetable oils come from seeds and nuts

Key Experiences

- Analyzing: separating and measuring the parts of a mixture or material to describe its composition
- Looking at familiar things in a new way
- Comparing the properties of materials

Materials

For each pair of children: some dried seeds—e.g., corn kernels, soybeans (not defatted), and some shelled nuts—peanuts, walnuts, cashews; a brown paper bag; a sturdy spoon, or a hammer, or pliers; an eye dropper; small amounts of vegetable oil and of water, garlic presses (optional)

Activity

Children first drop a few drops of oil on brown paper and also a few drops of water on brown paper, to see the characteristics of an oil stain versus a water stain. Then, wrapping each kind of seed (nut) in a small amount of brown paper, they use a spoon, pliers, or hammer to press, or crush it to see what kind of stain it produces. They might also try using a garlic press to squeeze a few drops of oil from an oily nut (e.g., a walnut).

Oil is one of the many products extracted from plants for human use. Many vegetable oils, such as corn, soybean, sunflower, and peanut oils, come from the seeds of plants. (Some, such as olive and palm oils, come from the fruits of plants.) One way to extract the oil, as this activity shows, is by pressing the seeds. Another method—soaking the seeds in a solvent to dissolve the oil and then evaporating the solvent out of the oil-solvent mixture—is used in some large-scale manufacturing processes.

Questions to Ask

On brown paper, how does a water stain look? How does it feel? How does this compare with an oil stain? What happens when you press or squeeze seeds (nuts) against brown paper? Where does the oil come from? How many corn kernels (or some other type of seed) would it take to fill a cup with oil? How do we use oil like this?

Extension

1. Children cook or bake something (e.g., cookies or muffins) using a recipe that calls for vegetable oil. They also try eliminating the oil from the recipe to see how the final product differs when no oil is used.

2. Children investigate labels of food products at home to see which ones contain vegetable oils.

Related Reading

Fenton, Carroll Lane, & Kitchen, Herminie B. *Plants That Feed Us* (pp 81, 84). New York: The John Day Co., 1956.

Selsam, Millicent E. *Play With Plants* (pp. 15–18). New York: William Morrow & Co., 1978.

Weiner, Michael A. *Man's Useful Plants* (pp. 30–32). New York: Macmillan Publishing Co. 1976.

Grades 2–3

How Much Is Water?

Seeing that water is a major constituent of plant life

Key Experiences

- Analyzing: separating and measuring the parts of a mixture or material to describe its composition
- Measuring properties and changes using standard or nonstandard units
- Observing and describing a pattern of change

Materials

For each small group of children: fruits and vegetables (e.g., green pepper, tomato, potato, carrot, banana, apple)—enough so each child can have a few slices to dehydrate; a pan balance or small spring scale; a dehydrator (or an oven)

Activity

Children slice off fruit and vegetable pieces and then weigh the slices. After drying the slices in a dehydrator overnight, they weigh the slices again and compare the weights before and after dehydration. (A household oven can also be used to dehydrate the slices if it is set very low and left open a crack so air can circulate over the drying slices. With an oven, an overnight period or more may be required for dehydration.)

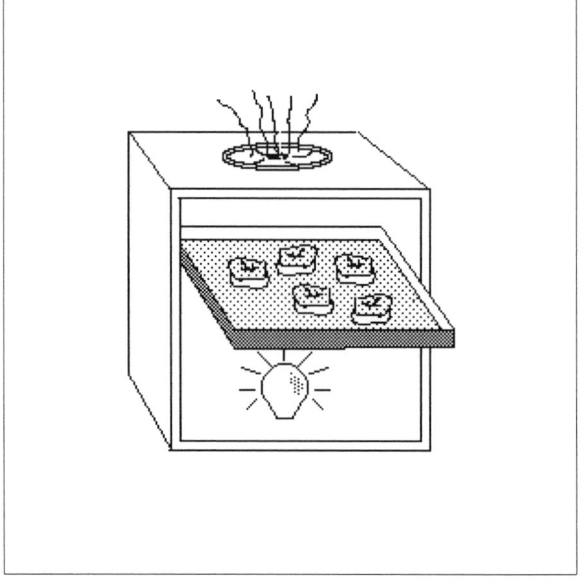

This activity can help children understand that water is a major component of living material, in this case, plant material. In fact, much of the living tissues of plants *and* animals is simply water—more than 75 percent in most plants and even a greater proportion in some animals.

Questions to Ask

How much did the slices weigh before drying? After drying? What was removed from the fruit? Why do you think so? What remains after the slices have been dehydrated? Where do you think the remaining material comes from?

Extension

1. Children try rehydrating the slices by soaking them in water overnight, to see if they return to their original condition.

2. Children read about drying of food as an early method of preservation.

3. Children investigate commercially available dried fruits and vegetables, learn how they are dried and how they are used.

Related Reading

Fenton, Carroll Lane, & Kitchen, Herminie B. *Plants That Feed Us* (pp.27–29). New York: The John Day Co., 1956.

Grimm, William C. *Indian Harvests* (pp. 75, 82, 84–85). New York: The John Day Company, 1956.

Weiner, Michael A. *Man's Useful Plants* (pp. 45, 54, 55). New York: Macmillan Publishing Co., 1976.

Grades K–2

Sugar From Plants

Discovering that sugar is a constituent of plant life

Key Experiences

- Analyzing: separating and measuring the parts of a mixture or material to describe its composition
- Observing and describing a pattern of change
- Comparing the properties of materials

Materials

For each small group: pieces of sugar cane and/or sugar beet; small cups; a dehydrator; refined sugar in a dish or in cubes; a garlic press; maple syrup

Activity

Children cut up the cane and the beets and use the garlic press to squeeze juice from the pieces, collecting the juice in small cups. After tasting some of the juice, they place the remainder in the dehydrator, along with a sample of maple syrup, until the moisture has evaporated and only sugar remains. They can then taste this and compare it with refined sugar.

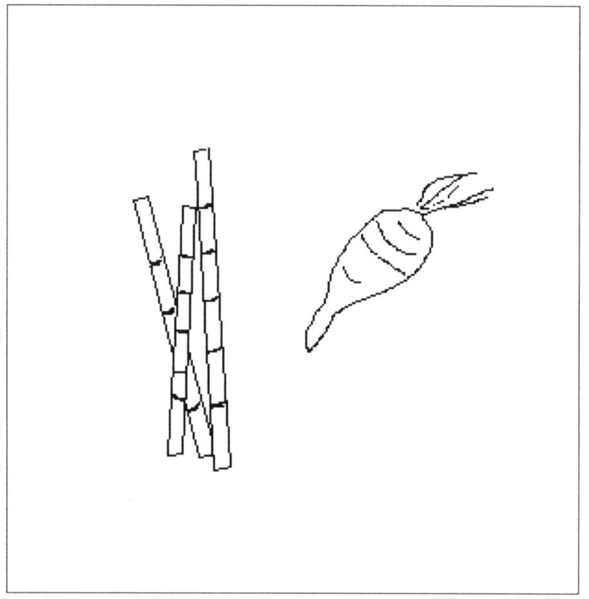

Sugar is an important product that comes from plants. Nearly all plants produce sugar, but a few, like sugar cane and sugar beets, produce it in such quantities that they have become valuable sources of the sweetener.

Questions to Ask

How does the juice of the cane (beet) taste? What else do you know of that tastes like this? What do you think is in cane (beet) juice to give it that taste? When you taste the material left after dehydrating, how does it taste? How much cane (or how many beets) do you think it would take to make a cup of sugar?

Extension

1. Children research to learn the many uses for sugar beets and sugar beet products.

2. Children visit a sugar maple grove to observe the process of tapping the trees and making maple syrup and maple sugar.

3. Children investigate the sugar content of other familiar fruits and vegetables.

Related Reading

Lasky, Kathryn. *Sugaring Time*. New York: MacMillan, 1983. (Making maple sugar)

Rahn, Joan Elma. *Grocery Store Botany* ("Roots," pp. 6–10). New York: Atheneum, 1974.

Weiner, Michael A. *Man's Useful Plants* (pp. 39–43). New York: Macmillan Publishing Co., Inc., 1976.

Grades 2–3

Plant Solids

Investigating the solid material in plants

Key Experiences

- Analyzing: separating and measuring the parts of a mixture or material to describe its composition
- Repeating an activity that produces change to gain awareness of possible causes
- Identifying more than one possible cause for a change

Materials

For each small group: potting soil, planting trays, grass seed (e.g., rye grass), a dehydrator (one for the whole class), a balance or small spring scale, liquid plant fertilizer (optional)

Activity

Children use potting soil in planting trays to plant a crop of grass. They then provide the trays with light and water to make the grass grow. (Adding liquid fertilizer can improve the growth rate.) As it grows, they harvest (cut) it on a regular basis and dehydrate the clippings, weighing them (and recording the weights) both before and after dehydration. If they accumulate the dried material, it will soon become obvious that the small amount of seed they started with produces a comparatively large quantity of solid material.

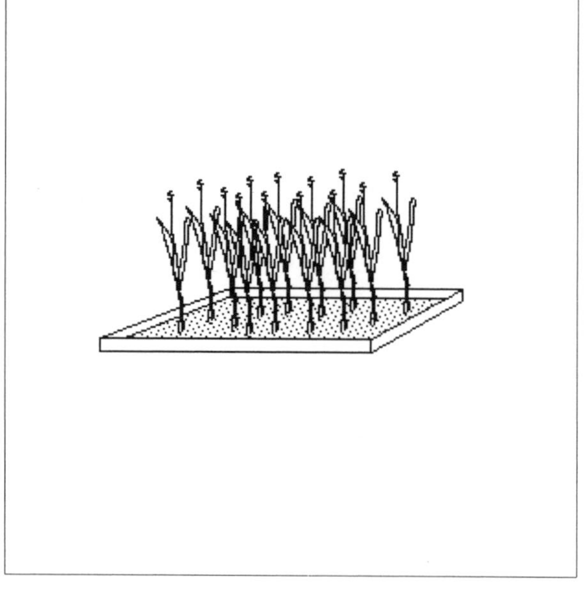

This activity emphasizes that growing plants contain solid material, in addition to water, and that in fact, they can generate great quantities of solid material without an appreciable change in the amount of soil they are growing in. While many children may feel that the solid material in plants is somehow "converted soil," this is not so. Plants are able to create dry material out of water and air—through the process of photosynthesis—while using only minute amounts of nutrients from the soil. It is not expected that children, at this stage, will understand photosynthesis, but they *can* come to appreciate the great quantity of solid material produced by these plants growing in only a small amount of soil.

Questions to Ask

What do you find when you compare the weight of the clippings before and after dehydrating them? How long do you think you could keep on harvesting grass clippings from your "lawn in a tray"? How do you think adding fertilizer affects the amount of clippings you are able to harvest? What other things does the grass need to keep putting out new growth? As you collect clippings week after week, does the amount of soil in the tray seem to be disappearing? If the grass is producing more and more clippings every week, and the soil seems to stay the same, where do you think the solid material in the clippings is coming from?

Extension

1. Children try varying the amount of sunlight on a tray of grass, or the amount of watering, or the amount of fertilizer, and keep records of harvest amounts for grass grown under the various conditions.

2. Children grow a tray of grass and harvest the clippings regularly to provide food for a small animal in the classroom.

3. Children further examine water/plant interaction by observing the process of *transpiration*—plants taking up water through their roots and then expelling it through their leaves. (For this, they need two bottles, both partly but equally filled with water. One bottle should have a plant cutting inserted through the neck of the bottle, which is then sealed with clay. The top of the plant should be enclosed in a transparent plastic bag, which can be fastened with a rubber band around the neck of the bottle. They can then observe how the water level in the plant's bottle changes and how the water reappears in the plastic bag, in the form of condensation.) They investigate how this process is affected by the bottle being in a cool place, in a warm place, in a light place, in a dark place, and so on. The plantless bottle, also sealed with clay, is a "comparison" bottle, whose water level remains practically the same throughout the activity, since no plant is taking up the water.

Children can further examine water/plant interaction by observing the process of transpiration.

Related Reading

Pringle, Laurence. *Being a Plant* (pp. 10–15). New York: Thomas Y. Crowell, 1983.

Rahn, Joan Elma. *Watch It Grow, Watch It Change* (pp. 68–71). New York: Atheneum, 1978.

Selsam, Millicent E. *Play With Plants* (pp. 11–16. 31–34). New York: William Morrow & Co., 1978.

Grades 1–3

An Earthworm Farm

Discovering what earthworms take from and give to the environment

Key Experiences

- Observing and describing a pattern of change
- Building environments for living things

Materials

A dozen red worms (they are easier to raise than night crawlers) from outdoors or from a bait shop; a large plastic dish or tub (with sides 4 in.–6 in. high); loam soil, peat, and leaf mulch; worm food (corn meal or ground oatmeal, a tablespoon scattered over the soil every month)

Activity

Children construct an earthworm farm by placing starter worms in a dish of moistened soil and covering the dish with a cloth to retain moisture. Periodically, they loosen the soil by sifting it with their hands or with a small stick, check the moisture, count the number of worms, and watch for cocoons (a little smaller than an apple seed) or newly hatched worms (after 3–4 weeks).

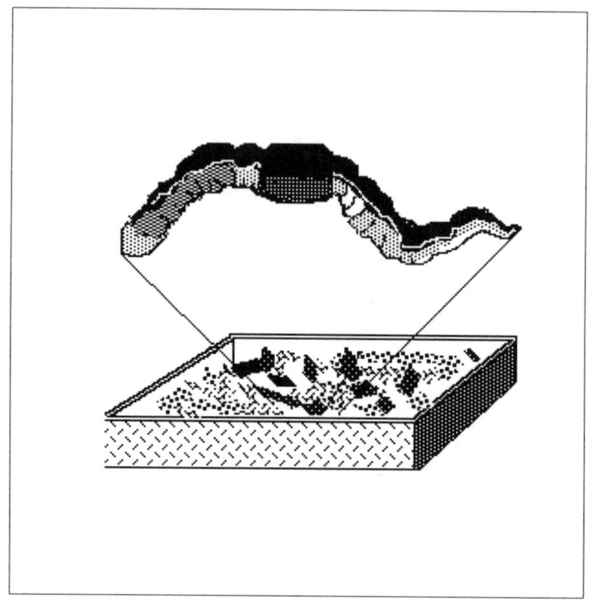

Since the earthworm's needs and behavior are rather easy to observe, it is a good animal for children to study to identify the environmental factors affecting a life cycle. As the worms swallow the soil, they leave behind casts enriched in nutrients valuable to plants. When earthworms live in the soil of a lawn or garden, they lighten and break up the soil and add nutrients to it by producing the casts.

Questions to Ask

How many worms did the farm start with? What do you notice about the number of worms as time goes on? What things make up the earthworm's environment? What does the earthworm take from the environment? What does the earthworm give to the environment? When or where do you most often find earthworms (besides a bait shop)?

What evidence do they leave behind in a lawn or garden? When earthworms live in a garden or lawn, why do you think they burrow down into the soil? What happens when you try to push your finger down into the ground? How do you think such a soft-bodied animal as the earthworm is able to burrow down into solid ground?

Extension

1. Children, for a short time, observe an earthworm on a piece of white paper, noting whether it has eyes, ears, a mouth, legs, and so on. They note the sensitivity of the body, the sensitivity to light, the rings and segments on the body, the transparency of the skin, the thick ring in the middle of the body (this contains the glands that make its egg cocoons). Listening very carefully, they hear a faint scraping or rustling sound (made by the small bristles on the worm's underside—easily seen with a magnifying glass).

2. Children find a patch of ground outdoors that has earthworm casts on it, mark out a small area on it, and sweep up and weigh the casts from this area over a period of several days. They observe when the casts are typically made, in what weather conditions, and so on. They also try growing seeds in accumulated cast soil and in ordinary soil, to see which is the richest soil for plants.

Related Reading

Hess, Lilo. *The Amazing Earthworm.* New York: Charles Scribner's Sons, 1979.

Lauber, Patricia. *Earthworms, Underground Farmers.* Champaign, IL: Garrard Publishing Co., 1976.

McLaughlin, Molly. *Earthworms, Dirt, and Rotten Leaves: An Exploration in Ecology.* New York: Atheneum, 1986.

Patent, Dorothy Hinshaw. *The World of Worms.* (pp. 76–81). New York: Holiday House, 1978.

Washburn, George N. *The Care and Culture of Earthworms* (Fish Division pamphlet No. 34). Lansing, MI: Michigan Department of Conservation, March, 1961.

Grades K–3

Human Growth and Change

Studying evidence of human growth

Key Experiences

- Observing changes over time
- Ordering objects according to variation along a single dimension
- Reporting and representing observations

Materials

Paper and markers for tracing

Activity

Each child traces outlines of both hands or both feet and labels them with his or her name. The children within a small group use the outlines of one hand or foot (e.g., everyone's right hand) to create a display of the outlines ordered according to size. The outlines of their other (left) hands or feet are stored in a safe place, so the tracing activity can be repeated in the second half of the year and children can compare early and later tracings to detect growth.

Human change, although it occurs very slowly compared to that of earthworms, is an excellent topic for children because they can begin by studying themselves. Human growth can be detected by keeping careful records—like the pencil marks on a wall that families use to record a child's increasing height.

Questions to Ask

In your group, are everyone's hands the same size, or are there different-sized hands? How does your hand size now compare with your hand size when you were a baby? How does your hand size now compare to that of an adult? If you trace your hand again at (some specific future time) what do you think you will find has happened between now and then? How much do you think your hand will grow between now and then? What are some other signs of your growth that we could watch for between now and then? How could we make records to help us detect that growth? What are some of the things that cause you to grow? Besides growing larger, what are some other ways you have changed since you were a baby? What are some other ways you will change in the future?

Extension

1. Children record their heights on a large chart early in the year, and then later in the year. They also use a piece of string to record head size (circumference), arm length, and so on, for later comparisons.

2. Children learn about the length of time various creatures take to grow to adult size—birds, dogs, elephants, humans—and make a graph to show the comparisons.

3. Children bring pictures of themselves when they were infants or toddlers and observe the ways they have changed from then to now.

4. Children experience how human change can be brought about by practice, as well as growth. For example, they practice such skills as a ring toss or rope jumping and keep records over several days to show how they improve.

Related Reading

Balestrine, P. *The Skeleton Inside You.* New York: Thomas Y. Crowell Co., 1971.

Elgin, Kathleen. *The Hand.* New York: Franklin Watts, Inc., 1968.

Rothenberg, Robert, M.D. *Growing Up Healthy, What Goes On Inside Us.* New York: The Danbury Press, Walt Disney Productions, 1975.

Grades 2–3

A Litter Survey

Analyzing the build-up of unwanted materials in the human environment

Key Experiences

- Analyzing: separating and measuring the parts of a mixture to describe its composition
- Classifying materials into small groups based on common attributes
- Using bar graphs

Materials

Litter collection bags for each pair of children; plastic gloves for each child; materials for making a graph

Activity

Working in pairs and wearing plastic gloves for safety, children visit an outdoor area (playground, park) and gather litter. (Children are warned not to collect any broken glass.) Then they decide what different categories of litter they have, and after sorting the litter into these categories, they create graphs comparing the incidence of various types of litter.

This activity points up how the beauty of the human environment can be upset by the build-up of unwanted materials.

Questions to Ask

Why do we consider some things to be litter in our environment? What different kinds of groups did you sort your litter into? What type of litter did you find the most of? The least of? Can you think of any reasons for this? What happens to litter if no one picks it up? Who leaves litter behind? What can you tell about the lives of those who have left this litter?

Extension

1. Children investigate alternatives to littering. They learn about recyclables and biodegradeables, about landfills and recycling centers.

2. Children collect and analyze litter from other environments, such as the school hallways or the school cafeteria. They also choose to help beautify an area of the school building or grounds by analyzing and then dispos-

ing of all the litter and then mounting a campaign to reduce the most predominate type of litter.

Related Reading

Pringle, Laurence. *Throwing Things Away* (pp. 8, 11, 16–17, 28). New York: Thomas Y. Crowell, 1986.

Shuttlesworth, Dorothy, & Cervasio, Thomas. *Litter: The Ugly Enemy, An Ecology Story*. New York: Doubleday, 1973.

Weiss, Malcolm E. *Toxic Waste* ("The Good Old Days," pp. 9–14). New York: Franklin Watts, Inc., 1984.

Grades K–3

Surveying Life—Land and Sea

Sampling an area to discover what lives in an environment

Key Experiences

- Classifying and ordering materials according to their attributes and properties
- Using identification guides
- Using bar graphs

Materials

Identification books for shells, birds, insects, wildflowers, sea animals, trees; equipment for drawing, graph making

Activity

On a regular basis, or for a definite length of time, children observe a defined area—a weed patch, a grove of trees, a bird feeder, a tidal pool, a part of a beach or shoreline—depending on what is accessible. They keep records of the signs of plant or animal life they see there (collect and identify shells, count and identify wild flowers, count and identify forms of sea life, collect and identify fallen leaves from trees, count and identify birds). They use these records, and perhaps drawings of the forms of life they observe but cannot collect, to make graphs showing how commonly (or frequently) the particular form of tree, plant, or animal life is observed.

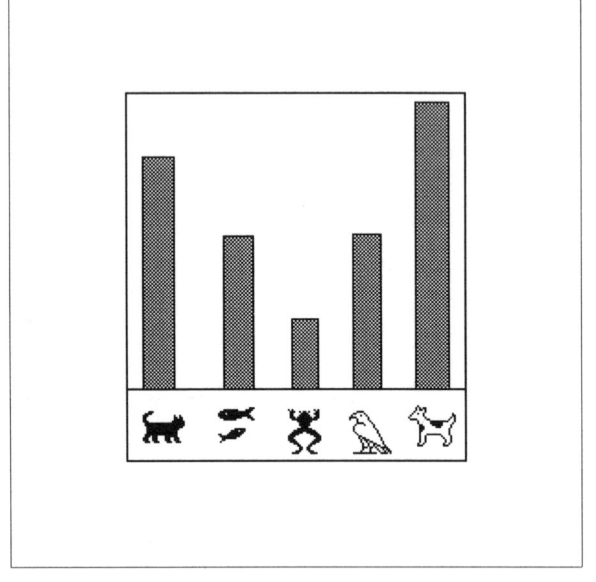

Questions to Ask

What forms of life (plant, tree, sea, insect, etc.) did you choose to survey? Where did you make your survey? Can you describe some things about the environment you surveyed? How often (or how long) did you observe your area? What different kinds of plant (animal) life did you find? What kinds of samples did you collect? How did you identify them? Were there any you couldn't identify? Can you describe them? What did you see (find) the most of? The least of? Can you think of features of the environment you surveyed that would explain why (a certain plant or creature) is frequently found there? Why might people find surveys of plant or animal or sea life useful?

Extension

Children learn about the role environmental counts play in determining that a species is endangered. They also think of ways they could help to preserve an endangered species. (The closer these examples are to home, the better.)

Related Reading

Kohl, Judith & Herbert. *The View from the Oak* (Sierra Club Books). San Francisco: Charles Scribner's Sons, 1977.

Pringle, Laurence. *Into the Woods*. New York: Macmillan Publishing Co., 1973.

Pringle, Laurence. *This Is a River*. New York: Macmillan Publishing Co., 1972.

Ross, Wilda. *Cracks and Crannies, What Lives There*. New York: Coward, McCann, & Geoghegan, Inc., 1975.

8

▼

Structure and Form

Grades K–1

Sorting Shells

Investigating the structure of shells

Key Experiences

- Observing similarities and differences
- Observing color, shape, form, and pattern
- Observing similarities and differences in structural patterns and grouping objects accordingly

Materials

For each pair of children: an assortment of seashells (collected from the beach or purchased) and several sorting trays or mats

Activity

Children use sorting trays or mats to sort shells into categories of their choosing (fan-shaped, two-part, spiral, and so on). Within each category, they might choose to arrange the shells according to size or color. In the process of sorting, the children will need to look at the shells' patterns, shapes, and structural forms.

Children love collecting and sorting the shells they have found, but freshly collected shells should be washed well in hot water several times to remove their smell. Shells that look a bit dull and colorless when dry may be improved by rubbing lightly with clear mineral oil or baby oil.

Questions to Ask

How did you arrange your shells? What colors do you see in the shells? What patterns do you see? Do some shells have similar patterns? Can you see patterns inside of any shells (particularly if some shells are broken open)? What purpose do shells serve?

Extension

Children use shell identification books to find pictures of their shells and learn their common names. Then they make a display of labeled shells.

Related Reading

Gutnik, Martin J. *Science of Classification: Finding Order Among Living and Nonliving Objects*. New York: Franklin Watts, 1980.

Parker, Bertha Morris. *Pebbles and Sea Shells*. Evanston, IL: Row, Peterson & Co., 1959.

Romashko, Sandra. *The Shell Book*. Miami, FL: Windwood Publishing, Inc., 1984.

Simon, Hilda. *Snails of Land and Sea*. New York: The Vanguard Press, Inc., 1976.

Grades K–1

Sorting Leaves

Investigating leaf structure

Key Experiences

- Observing similarities and differences in structural patterns and grouping objects accordingly
- Arranging collections or displays to present findings

Materials

Children's collections of a variety of fall leaves; sorting trays or mats for each child

Activity

Children make a trip to a woods or park to collect fallen leaves, with each child collecting his or her own assortment of leaves. Then they make tracings (or rubbings) of the different kinds of leaves, sort the tracings (or rubbings) into groups according to shape, and label the groups with names they have made up to describe the shapes.

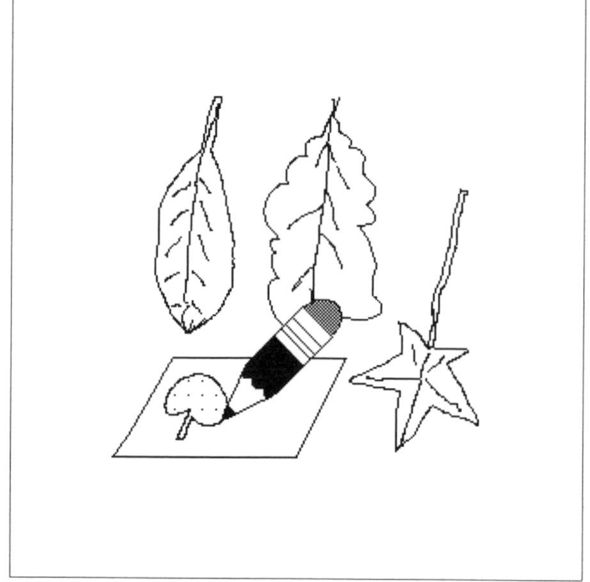

Encourage children to collect moist leaves rather than dry leaves, so the leaves can bend without breaking (this will help in tracing). Tracing is used to help children focus on the forms of the leaves—their overall shape and their edges—since that is the central idea of this activity. At another time, other sorting and classifying activities can focus on color, size, and other attributes of the leaves. Technical names have been developed for many leaf forms, and some of these may be introduced, but only after children have invented their own descriptive names for the leaf forms.

Questions to Ask

How many different kinds of leaves have you found? What ways did you group the leaves? How could you describe the leaves you put in each group?

Extension

1. Children use spatter painting to create a class mural of leaf shapes. In the mural, they use groupings of leaves, or patterns of leaves ordered by shape and size, as illustrations of structural variation in leaves.

2. Children use a leaf identification book to label leaf types.

3. Children make tracings of leaves on squared paper and count the squares to compare the areas of various kinds of leaves.

4. Children sort leaves by their types of vein patterns. The patterns are especially evident from leaf rubbings.

5. Children investigate their leaves for evidence of leaf eaters. This leads to a discussion of who eats leaves, what kinds of leaves humans eat, and so on.

Related Reading

Hutchins, Ross E. *This Is a Leaf.* New York: Dodd, Mead & Co., 1962.

Lerner, Sharon. *I Found a Leaf.* Minneapolis, MN: Lerner Publications, 1964.

Wohlrabe, Raymond A. *Exploring the World of Leaves.* New York: Thomas Y. Crowell Company, 1976.

Grades K–2

Cabbage—A Big Bud

Investigating the layered structure of a bud

Key Experiences

- Taking something apart to observe it more closely
- Observing similarities and differences in structural patterns

Materials

For each pair of children: a wedge of cabbage (about 1/8 of a cabbage), some other large bud (for example, a gladiola bud), a stiff sheet of paper to use as mounting material, clear tape; for the whole group: a half-cabbage for observation and comparison

Activity

Children investigate bud structure by taking apart the thin wedge of cabbage, layer by layer, and taping onto paper the pulled-off pieces in the order they are removed. As they do so, they can compare the dissected layers with the layers in the half-cabbage.

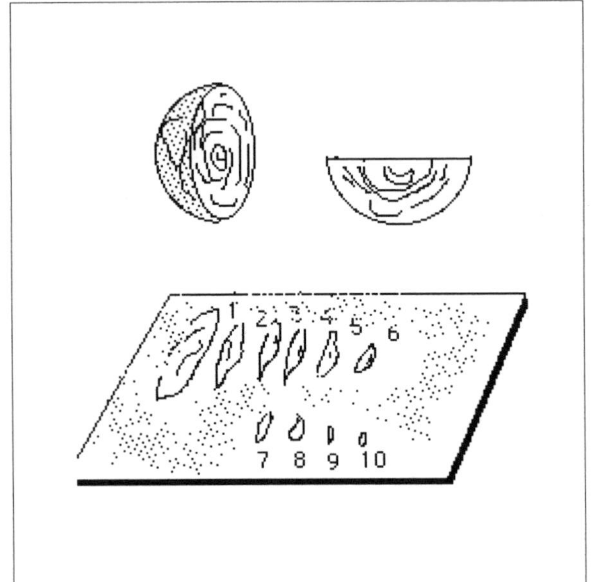

After dissecting the cabbage (which is a leaf bud), they can do the same with a smaller bud (perhaps a flower bud) and compare the kinds of layers found in each of the buds.

If you inspect almost any bare tree or bush in winter, you will see leaf buds on the twigs. Likewise, in spring and summer, flower buds can be observed on many flowering plants. Children can realize that a bud contains and protects the undeveloped shoot, leaf, or flower of a plant if they are able to observe the structure of the bud and the sequence of steps through which a bud unfolds.

Questions to Ask

How would you describe the outer layer of the cabbage bud? Of the flower bud? How many layers did you find in each of your buds? What purpose do you think buds serve? If a bud goes on growing, what do you think happens? How are the cabbage and smaller bud alike? How are they different?

Extension

Children take a walk to observe winter, spring, or summer buds, comparing their shapes, and colors, the pattern they form on stems, the numbers of layers on each, and the arrangement of the layers. If opened and unopened buds exist on the same plant, they compare the closed bud to its final form.

Related Reading

Rahn, Joan Elma. *Grocery Store Botany* (pp. 25–28). New York: Atheneum, 1974.

Rahn, Joan Elma. *Watch It Grow, Watch It Change* (pp. 7–32). New York: Atheneum, 1978.

Zim, Herbert S. *What's Inside a Plant.* New York: William Morrow & Co., 1952.

Grades 1–2

Seed Patterns

Discovering that seeds form unique patterns in fruits and vegetables

Key Experiences

- Observing color, shape, form, and pattern
- Looking at familiar things in a new way

Materials

For each pair of children: a variety of fresh fruits and vegetables containing seeds (apple, pear, lime, kiwi, cucumber, tomato, zucchini, avocado, grape, strawberry) and also some nuts (almond, hazelnut, acorn); a knife and a small saw (optional)

Activity

Children cut fruit, vegetables, and nuts open to examine the seed pattern or the inside structure (in the case of nuts). They may need your assistance in splitting the nuts open (or sawing them in half). Some fruits or vegetables, if children cut them in different ways, will reveal different cross-sectional seed patterns. The tomato and apple are good examples of this.

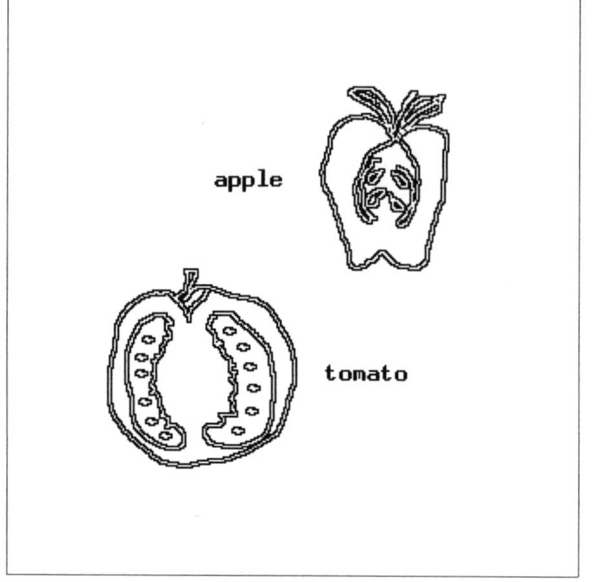

After observing the various seed patterns, children might display and label the different kinds of seeds.

Though this activity involves certain "fruits, vegetables, and nuts," strictly speaking these are all the same part, the "fruit" of the growing plant—the structure that contains the plant's seed(s). These have developed from the ovary of the flower after pollination. Sometimes the outer wall of the ovary becomes fleshy, as in the apple or cucumber. Other times, the ovary wall stays hard (the shell of a nut is an example of this). In both cases, the outer part of the ovary protects the seeds.

Seeds are often contained within the fruit, as in apples, oranges, and some nuts (walnuts and almonds). Sometimes, however, they are on the outside of the fruit (strawberry seeds are an example).

Questions to Ask

Can you find the part of the fruit (or vegetable or nut) that we eat? Is the pattern of seeds the same no matter which way you make the cut? How many seeds are there? What is the purpose of the fleshy part of the fruit (or vegetable)?

Extension

1. Children make an expedition to a wooded area or park to collect seeds of wild and garden plants (for example, dandelion, thistle, or poppy seeds). Putting a plastic bag over the head of a flower before cutting the stem is a useful technique for collecting some fragile seeds.

2. Children make a collection of empty seed cases from wild and garden plants.

3. Children discuss who eats seeds and what seeds humans eat. Children investigate which seeds dominate the diets of peoples in various regions of the world, an activity that can tie in with many themes in social studies.

Related Reading

Bjork, Christina, & Anderson, Lena. *Linnea's Windowsill Garden.* Stockholm: Rabin & Sjogren, 1978, translated 1988.

Rahn, Joan Elma. *Grocery Store Botany.* New York: Atheneum, 1974.

Selsam, Millicent E. *Seeds and More Seeds.* New York: Harper & Row Publishers, Inc., 1956.

Zim, Herbert S. *What's Inside a Plant.* New York: William Morrow & Co., 1952.

Grades K–2

Analyzing Mixtures

Sorting a mixture into its components and comparing quantities of the different components

Key Experiences

- Analyzing: separating and measuring the parts of a mixture or material to describe its composition
- Looking at familiar things in a new way

Materials

For each pair of children: a small amount of some mixture to sort (e.g., birdseed, mixed dried fruit, cereal with raisins, mixed nuts, hard candy assortment); materials for making a display showing the make-up of their mixture

Activity

Children determine the different components of their mixture by sorting. Then they display the results of their sorting in some way to show the comparative quantities of the various materials in the mixture.

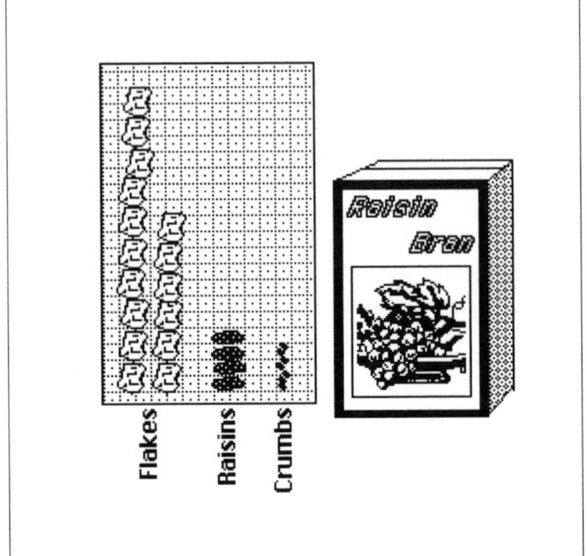

Sorting of this type is a simple form of quantitative analysis, which is one method of determining the composition and hence the desirability of common products we might want to buy.

Questions to Ask

How many different kinds of things did you find in your mixture? What thing did you find the most of? The least of? How did you make a display to show the composition of your mixture? When might it be helpful for you to know the composition of a mixture like the one you analyzed?

Extension

Children analyze and compare the composition of two different brands of some product—bird seed, or raisin bran, for example—and decide which would be better to buy and for what reasons.

Related Reading

Wyler, Rose. *Science Fun With Mud and Dirt.* Morristown, NJ: Messner, 1986. (Section on sorting dirt particles)

Grades 1–3

A Yardstick Balance

Making and using a balance for comparing weights

Key Experiences

- Using plans supplied by others to make more complex and functional structures
- Measuring properties and changes using standard or nonstandard whole units

Materials

For each pair of children: an inexpensive wooden yard or meter stick, two plastic sandwich bags, paper clips, string or yarn

Activity

Children construct a simple balance, as shown, by hanging plastic bags from two ends of a stick that is able to pivot on an axis (a loop of string). To use the balance, children hold it by the central loop of string or tie the string to a table or chair, so that the balance pivots freely. Then they explore putting small objects (e.g., two Matchbox cars, two blocks, two walnuts, two cookies) in the cups to see if they weigh the same or if one is heavier than the other.

To make up for slight imperfections in the distribution of weight in the balance itself, children can initially level the balance by moving the loop of string until the scale balances.

This balance is useful for comparing two things to see which is heavier. It can also be used to compare an object with some type of unit weights (standard or nonstandard). For example, using large paper clips as units of weight, children might balance something against the paper clips, adding one at a time, and thus determine that it weighs more than 2 paper clips but less than 3.

Questions to Ask

How did you construct your balance? How does it work? Why is it important to figure out a way to make the stick level to start with? What does it mean if the stick stays level when you put something in each cup? What does it mean when one end of the stick goes down? What kinds of things did you compare with your balance? Were there some things that you could not use your balance to compare? Why? How could you make a balance to compare them? How could you make a better balance?

Extension

1. Children figure out how to use a coat hanger to make a balance for comparing weights.

2. Children use the balance in analyzing mixtures (as in the previous activity) weighing cereal samples of equal volume, for example, to see which mixture has more raisins.

3. Children try to estimate an object's weight in some kind of units (guessing "how many paper clips it weighs," for example) and then use the scale to actually compare it to paper clips.

Related Reading

Pine, Tillie, & Levine, Joseph. *Measurements, And How We Use Them.* New York: McGraw-Hill Book Co., 1977.

Russell, Solveig P. *Size, Distance, Weight.* New York: Henry Z. Walck, Inc., 1968.

Srivastova, Jane. *Weighing and Balancing.* New York: Thomas Y. Crowell Co., 1970.

Grades 1–2

Sorting Papers

Examining variations in the properties of paper and relating them to structure

Materials

For each child, a set of 4 in. × 4 in. squares of noticeably different kinds of paper (newspaper, construction paper, glossy paper, kraft paper, facial tissue, wallpaper, waxed paper, etc.); a magnifying glass for each pair of children (optional)

Key Experiences

- Classifying materials into small groups based on common attributes
- Ordering objects according to variation along a single dimension
- Using instruments to assist observations

Activity

Children examine the paper samples and sort and re-sort them into groups, classifying or ordering them according to some property of their choice, such as thickness, weight, stiffness, roughness, opaqueness. Having all the samples the same size should help children, when they are sorting, to focus attention on properties like texture, transparency, and color. If they tear the edge of each sample and look at it with a magnifying glass, differences in the density and coarseness of the papers' fibers can be seen. After sorting, children can explain how they chose to sort the samples.

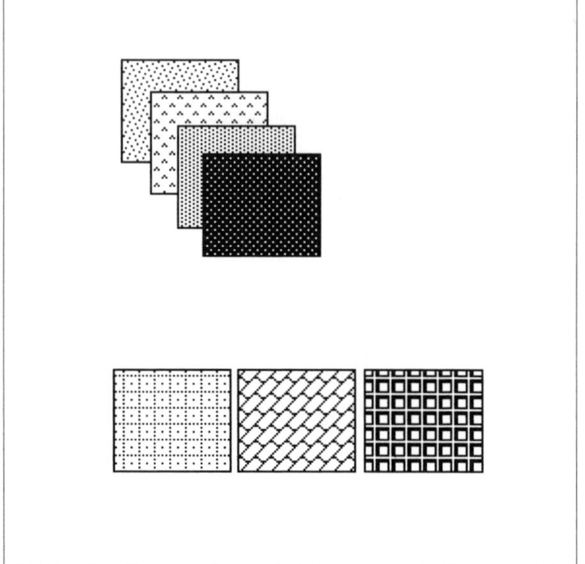

The great variety in kinds of paper provides an opportunity to observe differing manmade forms and to relate these forms to physical properties. Paper is made up of wood and other fibers matted together in sheets. The coarseness of the fibers, how tightly they are packed, and what other materials they are mixed with are the factors that determine whether the paper will be smooth or coarse, shiny or dull, and so on.

Questions to Ask

How did you choose to sort your papers? How are the papers different from one another? Can you tell something about the fibers in your different samples?

Extension

1. Children make a display showing their samples ordered according to the properties they chose.

2. Children look for additional kinds of paper samples and examine their structure and composition.

3. Children investigate materials people have used to write on throughout history—such as cave walls, animal skins, stones, parchment, and modern paper made from wood pulp—and relate writing methods and materials to other aspects of life in the societies they are studying.

Related Reading

Cosner, Sharon. *Paper Through the Ages.* Minneapolis, MN: Carolrhoda Books, 1984.

Fobbester, Jim. *Paper* (pp.32–43). Hove, East Sussex, England: Wayland Publishers Limited, 1980.

Grumer, Arnold E. *Paper by Kids.* Minneapolis, MN: Dillon Press, Inc., 1980.

Limosin, Odele. *The Story of Paper.* Ossing, NY: Young Discovery Library, 1988.

Grades 1–3

Testing Paper Strength

Relating tear strength of paper to paper structure

Key Experiences

- Testing: assessing properties by comparing effects of standardized procedures
- Increasing or decreasing a causal factor and comparing the effects produced

Materials

For each pair of children: a hole punch and two sets of 4 in. × 4 in. samples of various lightweight papers (tissue paper, writing paper, newspaper, toweling, facial tissue, wrapping paper, for example); one large metal paper clip; a small plastic bag; some set of uniform objects to use as "weights" (small wood or plastic blocks, dominoes, Legos, washers); a magnifying glass (optional); a water source

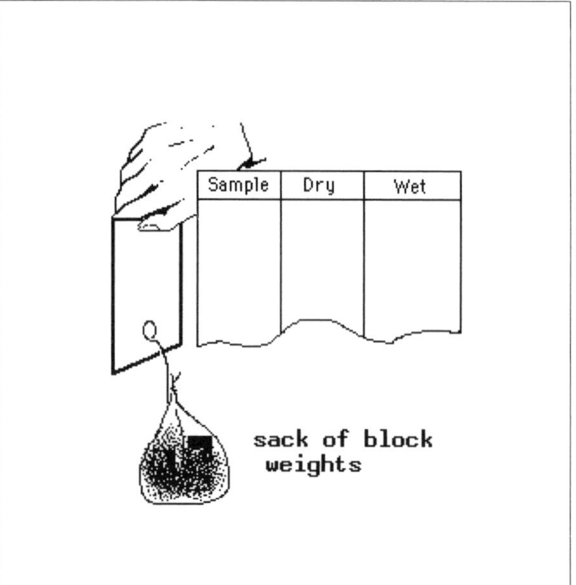

Activity

By hanging a bag of light weights from a hole in each paper sample (at least ½" from the edge), children test the various paper samples for their resistance to tearing. When the plastic bag is suspended with a paper clip "hook" as shown, and when children add the weights one by one, the hook will tear through the paper as soon as sufficient weight has been added.

Children can test both wet and dry samples of paper and record the number of weights needed to tear the paper in each case. They can also use a magnifying glass to compare the fibers and the composition of the various samples, once they know which are the strong and the weak ones.

A paper sample's resistance to tearing, unlike such properties as its color, texture, and weight, is not immediately obvious but can easily be determined by a test such as this. You will find that the types of paper samples you include in this activity will determine how lightweight your units of measure should be: If the units are too light, it may take too many of them to tear sturdy paper. If the units are too heavy, there may not be enough variation in the numbers needed to tear various delicate papers.

Questions to Ask

Which papers are strong and which are weak? How are the paper samples different? Why are some papers stronger than others? How can you strengthen paper?

Extension

1. Children try the tear-strength test after the hook holes have been reinforced with loose-leaf hole reinforcers.

2. Children test the same paper samples, but with two different sets of weight units (one fine and one gross), to see which kind of weight unit gives them the most useful information.

3. Children make paper from waste paper and rags to get insight into the relationship between paper's composition and its physical properties.

Related Reading

Burdette, Janet, et al. *The Manufacture of Pulp and Paper: Science and Engineering Concepts.* Atlanta, GA: Tappi, 1988.

Cook, Janet, & Bond, Shirley. *Where Things Come From and How Things Are Made.* Tulsa: EDC Publishing, 1989.

Fobbester, Jim. *Paper.* Hove, East Sussex, England: Wayland Publishers Limited, 1980.

Grumer, Arnold E. *Paper by Kids.* Minneapolis, MN: Dillon Press, Inc., 1980.

Grades 1–2

Testing Paper Absorbency

Relating absorbency of paper to paper's structure

Key Experiences

- Testing: assessing properties by comparing effects of standardized procedures
- Looking at familiar things in a new way
- Using bar graphs

Materials

For each pair of children, 2 in. × 2 in. squares of various absorbent papers—paper toweling, napkins, facial tissues, a small drinking cup to hold water, an eye dropper, a magnifying glass (optional), and a tray to contain spills

Activity

Children test the absorbency of each paper sample by adding drops of water, one at a time, to a spill tray and blotting them up, one at a time, until the paper sample will hold no more. The number of drops a sample will hold is a measure of its absorbency. Children can record and graph their results.

It is important that the size of the samples be the same, so children can relate absorbency differences to properties such as a sample's coarseness or thickness, rather than its size. Looking at the torn edge of each sample with a magnifying glass may help children tell more about how structure and absorbency are related.

Questions to Ask

Are there differences in absorbency for different paper samples? What differences in the samples might explain why one absorbs more than another?

Extension

1. Children apply a similar test to some papers that are not designed specifically for absorbency—writing paper, newspaper, wrapping paper—and to some papers specifically designed to be nonabsorbent—wax paper, freezer paper, erasable bond. Then they investigate what

makes these papers different from the absorbent ones they tested earlier.

2. Children explore these questions: How can you treat absorbent paper to make it less absorbent? (For example, you can use wax or crayon or oil.) How can you make nonabsorbent paper more absorbent? (For example, you can shred it or rough up the surface.)

3. Children explore the absorbency of substances other than paper (for example, various building materials—bricks, wood, concrete, wallboard, rocks). They set an object, slightly submerged, in a pan of colored water and then record how long the water takes to rise 1 in. up the object, 2 in. up the object, and so on. A "wall" of sugar lumps set in a shallow pan of colored water will illustrate how water can seep up through several courses of bricks.

Related Reading

Grumer, Arnold E. *Paper by Kids*. Minneapolis, MN: Dillon Press, Inc. 1980.

Fobbester, Jim. *Paper*. Hove, East Sussex, England: Wayland Publishers Limited, 1980.

Scarry, Richard. *What Do People Do All Day?* New York: Random House, 1968.

Grades 1–3

Working With Natural Fibers

Exploring uses for natural fibers

Key Experiences

- Designing and building simple structures
- Looking at familiar things in a new way

Materials

For each small group: reeds, long grasses, various flexible plant stems (e.g., vines); an old picture frame with nails placed at 1-in. intervals along two parallel sides (to use as a weaving loom); sturdy string or cord (for the warp threads)

Activity

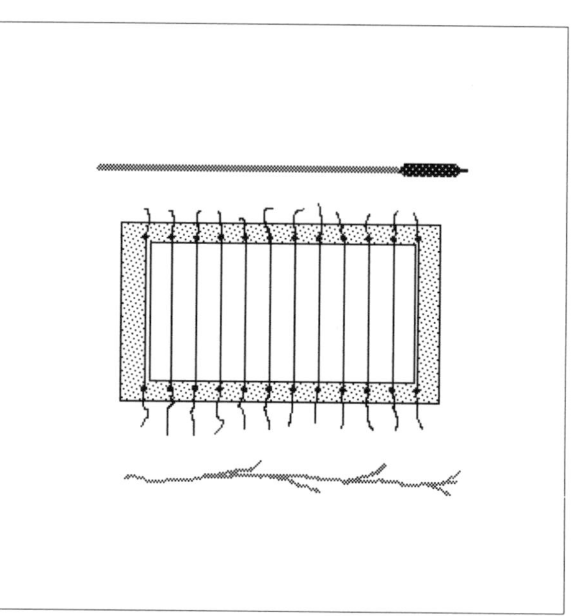

Children attach warp strings to the picture frame "loom" and then create a fabric mat. They do this by weaving natural fibers in and out among the strings, trimming off any projecting ends of the fibers, and then tying the warp strings to keep the fabric from coming apart. (The warp strings should have long enough ends left on them to allow adjacent ends of strings to be tied together in pairs.) By alternating the types of natural material used, and by braiding or twisting single strands together before weaving them in, they can create various patterns in their fabric.

Creating woven material through repetition of a structural pattern can lead to investigating the relationship between structure and form in other common uses of natural fibers.

Questions to Ask

What are some different ways you can weave a strand in and out through the warp strings? Besides using just one strand to weave at a time, what are some ways you might combine some strands before weaving them? What materials did you use in your weaving? Which materials worked best? Why? What pattern did you use in your weaving?

What are some things animals weave? What materials do they use in weaving? Does their weaving have a pattern? Besides mats like these, what are some other things that people weave? Are you wearing anything that is woven from plant materials? Is anything in your home or in the classroom woven from plant materials?

Extension

1. Children make a trip to a field in the spring or fall (when there is the least sap in stems) to collect natural materials to use in weaving.

2. Children investigate the structure of a woven basket and try to use natural materials to weave simple baskets.

3. Children study an abandoned bird's nest and take it apart to see what natural materials were used and what pattern there is to its construction.

4. Children investigate how cotton or linen fabric is made or how natural-fiber rope is made.

5. Children make a wall decoration on a vertical loom that is made by hanging individual warp strings (with weights tied to both ends) over a suspended rod.

Related Reading

Adler, Irving & Ruth. *Fibers.* New York: The John Day Co., 1964.

Buehr, Walter. *Cloth, From Fiber to Fabric.* New York, William Morrow & Co., 1965.

Cobb, Vicki. *Fuzz Does It.* New York: J. B. Lippincott, 1982.

Gilbreath, Alice. *Fun With Weaving.* New York: William Morrow & Co., 1976.

Grades 1–2

Fabric Fasteners

Investigating how mechanical cloth fasteners work

Key Experiences

- Comparing the performance of similar structures
- Taking something apart to observe it more closely

Materials

Fabric strips for making arm bands, head bands, and belts—enough so that each child can make something to wear; a variety of swatches (cut from old clothing) containing the matching parts of cloth fasteners (such as hooks and eyes, snap bases and studs, buttons and buttonholes, positive and negative Velcro) and easy-to-attach fasteners such as adhesive-backed Velcro (optional)—enough so that children have a choice of fasteners to use in making their "garments"; a stapler and a magnifying glass for each pair of children

Activity

Children staple the swatches to the ends of fabric strips to make themselves arm bands, head bands, and belts. To do this, they will have to match up the fastener parts that work together and decide how to position them to make them effective in fastening their garments. A hook and eye, for example, will work best if they are positioned in a way that puts sufficient tension on them. Velcro, on the other hand, allows more latitude in placement and is a good fastener when the size of a garment must be easily adjustable.

Looking at the separate parts of fasteners such as Velcro or the hook and eye with a magnifying glass will help children see how they work. Comparing one another's garments and how well they hold together will allow them to see the advantages and disadvantages of certain fasteners.

Questions to Ask

What do these fasteners do? How do they work? For certain fastening jobs, why do some fasteners work better than others? Are some easier to undo than others? What problems can you have with some of these fasteners? When would it be better to use these fasteners (the ones in this activity) instead of sewing or gluing two pieces of cloth together?

Extension

Children bring in other examples of ways to fasten clothing and investigate how they work (for example, toggles and loops, buckles, laces and eyelets). The zipper, though mechanically complicated, is a common example children want to discuss.

Related Reading

Gardner, Robert. *This Is the Way It Works* ("Zippers" on pp. 66-67). Garden City, NY: Doubleday & Co., Inc., 1980.

Macaulay, David. *The Way Things Work*. Boston: Houghton Mifflin Co., 1988.

Simons, Violet K. *Sewing, Altering, and Mending* ("Fastenings," pp. 52-64). New York: Sterling Publishing Co., Inc., 1976.

Grades 2–3

Waterproofing Fabric

Investigating the structure of waterproof fabrics

Key Experiences

- Improving a structure or material through trial-and-error modifications
- Testing: assessing properties by comparing effects of standardized procedures

Materials

For each pair of children: several 6 in. × 6 in. squares of cotton cloth (old shirt or handkerchief material); rubber bands; waterproofing materials—wax crayons, candle wax, salad oil, nail polish, foil wrap, thin plastic bag material or plastic wrap; glue; a small brush; an eyedropper; a glass or transparent plastic tumbler; a magnifying glass (optional)

Activity

Children first observe how drops of water dropped on a piece of cloth (stretched over the tumbler, as shown) soak into and pass through the cloth. Then they treat similar squares of cloth with various substances or materials and test each treated square for water resistance, dropping water on it with an eye dropper, again, as shown. (The waterproofing substances such as crayon, wax, oil, and polish can be rubbed or brushed on; the foil and plastic wrap can be glued to the fabric.) By holding the cloth up to the light or looking at it with a magnifying glass, children can examine each piece of cloth before and after waterproofing treatment.

Cotton fabric consists of fiber threads woven over and under one another. In most fabrics, not only do the threads themselves tend to absorb water, but the spaces between the threads allow water to pass through. Waterproofing substances or materials tend both to seal the fibers so they can't absorb water and to close up the spaces between the fibers so they can't allow water to pass through.

Questions to Ask

Before you waterproofed the cloth, what happened when you dropped water on it? Could you count the drops that penetrated, or fell through, the fabric? How can you explain why not all the drops fell through? What happened with the "water-drop test" after you treated the cloth with (crayon, oil, wax, and so on)? Which treatment(s) of the cloth turned out to be the best waterproofing)? When cloth is waterproof, what happens to water drops as they hit the surface of the cloth? If you hold up to the light some cloth that is not waterproof, what do you see? How is this different from what you see when the cloth is waterproof? What other ways can you think of to waterproof cloth? What do you think would work best for waterproofing clothing—can you explain why?

Extension

1. Children collect and test other substances for waterproofing.

2. Children try putting tiny pin holes in the foil wrap or plastic wrap and see if it still waterproofs cloth. (This is the basis of Gore-Tex water repellant fabric, i.e., it is perforated with holes large enough to let air and vapor, or sweat, pass through but small enough to resist water penetration).

Related Reading

Ardley, Neil. *Working With Water*. London: Franklin Watts, Inc., 1983.

Broekel, Ray. *Experiments With Water* (A New True Book). Chicago: Children's Press, 1988.

Catherall, Ed. *Adhesion*. Hove, East Sussex, England: Wayland Publishers Limited, 1983.

Grades 1–3

Stable and Unstable Structures

Exploring stability in two-dimensional hinged structures

Materials

Strips of tagboard, about ¾-in. wide and of various lengths, with holes punched at the ends—enough for each child to build several two-dimensional structures like those shown; brass fasteners for hinging them together

Key Experiences

- Designing and building simple structures
- Comparing the performance of similar structures
- Changing a structure to solve a problem in its design

Activity

Children use the fasteners and punched strips to design and build various two-dimensional hinged shapes. They experiment with making both closed structures (ones that have an inside and an outside space) and open structures. They experience the difference between structures that are stable (not flexible at the hinges) and ones that are unstable (flexible at the hinges). They identify these as "strong" and "weak," respectively.

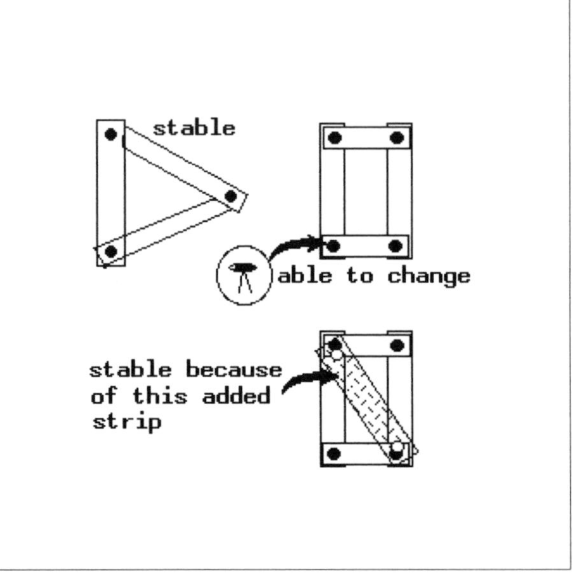

Some closed structures the children make will be simple (have just one inside space), while others will be complex (have several inside spaces). Among those with just one inside space (those that have just 3 sides and 3 corners, 4 sides and 4 corners, and so on), only one type—the triangle—will be stable. Of course, if children invent some complex closed structures that have one or more triangular shapes involved in them, these will also have some stability; but for children, the stability of the triangle is probably best pointed out with a simple triangle. This attribute of the triangular form makes it useful in such areas as bridge or building construction, where strength and rigidity are important.

Questions to Ask

How can you describe the shapes you have built? If you look at each shape, can you find an inside space? More than one inside space? If you built something with just one inside space, how many corners and how many sides does it have? Which closed shapes have corners that move? That can't move? If we compare all the strong shapes—the ones whose corners won't move, what can we say about them?

Extension

1. Children make a display of their two-dimensional structures, labeling them "strong" and "weak."

2. Children take structures that have just one inside space but various numbers of sides (squares, rectangles, pentagons, and so on) and experiment with ways to stabilize them by fastening more strips across the inside space. They need extra, unpunched tagboard strips, scissors, and a hole punch, so they can "tailor" the stabilizing strips to the task. Any strips that form a triangular area are, of course, stabilizing.

3. Children tour the school, looking for examples of triangles that stabilize structures in the classroom, the school building, and the play area—braces on gates, ceiling trusses, braces on desk or table legs, and spokes on bicycle wheels are a few examples.

4. Children make a display of pictures from magazines or catalogs showing triangles used in bridge construction, scaffolding, cranes, and so on.

Related Reading

Macaulay, David. *Castle.* Boston: Houghton Mifflin Co., 1977.

Stiles, David. *The Tree House Book.* New York: Avon Books, 1979.

Walker, Les. *House Building for Children.* Woodstock, NY: The Overlook Press, Inc., 1977.

Whyman, Kathryn. *Structures and Materials.* New York: Gloucester, 1987.

Grades 2–3

Building With Triangles

Using the triangular form in building miniature shelters

Materials

Drinking straws, or 8-in.–12-in. balsa wood sticks (1⁄8-in. × 1⁄8-in.), and small balls of clay—enough for each pair of children to build a few structures like those shown; string or rubber bands, wire ties, or thin hobby wire; tissue paper or cloth; scissors

Activity

Children experience using triangular forms in designing and building miniature housing structures such as tents and tepees.

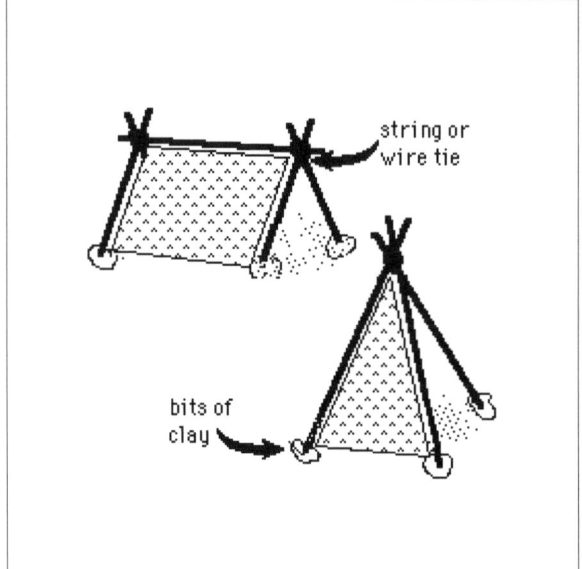

To support the buildings, they use straws or balsa wood sticks that are "footed" in small lumps of clay and joined at the top by twisted string, rubber bands, or wire. The structures can then be covered with tissue paper or cloth. (Building on construction paper sheets will allow structures to be preserved and moved.)

The triangles involved in tepees or tents will have two sides that are straws and a third "side" that is the building surface. Children may need help with this idea. To appreciate the advantage of a triangular support system, children might also explore what happens when they try to use the straws or sticks to make structures without triangles, for example, a four-legged table-shaped structure.

Questions to Ask

Can you point out the triangles you've used in your structure? Are there any places you could add a straw (or stick) to make your structure even more stable?

Key Experiences

Designing and building simple structures

Comparing the performance of similar structures

Extension

Children learn about the history and structure of Native American dwellings.

Related Reading

Grant, Bruce. *American Indians.* New York: E. P. Dutton & Co., Inc., 1960.

Simon, Nancy, & Wolfson, Evelyn. *American Indian Habitats.* New York: David McKay Co., Inc., 1978.

Yue, David, & Yue, Charlotte. *Tipi.* New York: Alfred A. Knopf, Inc., 1984.

Grade 3

Tower Building

Building lattice structures

Key Experiences

- Designing and building more complex structures
- Comparing the performance of similar structures
- Improving a structure or material through trial-and-error modifications

Materials

For each pair of children, 3-in. balsa wood sticks (plus some longer sticks that can be cut into lengths suitable for diagonal supports) and miniature marshmallows—enough for building a tower; scissors

Activity

Children use the 3" sticks, joined by marshmallows, to build lattice-type towers. They explore the advantages of using diagonal supports (forming triangles) in the tower construction.

One basic unit children might make with the 3" sticks is shown in the illustration (1). This unit can then be expanded into a cube (2). Joining several cubic units together produces a tower. In a similar way, starting with a triangle as the base, children can devise building units that are triangular prisms (4). With either basic building unit, it is possible to introduce stabilizing diagonal braces, as shown (3 and 4). For these braces, children will have to cut sticks longer than the 3" sticks you have provided. Determining the diagonal length can be done by trial and error or by crude "measuring."

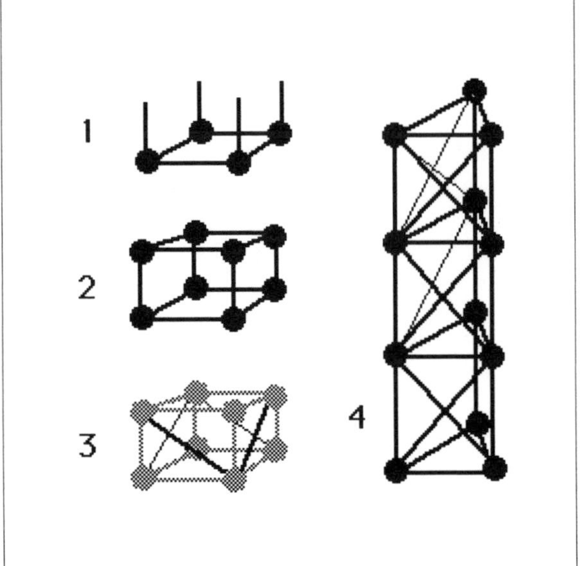

Questions to Ask

How high is your tower? How many sticks did you use? What happens if you leave out the diagonal braces?

Extension

1. Children also make structures such as bridges and houses with dried peas and toothpicks. The peas are first

soaked until soft enough to be pierced by the toothpicks. When left overnight to dry, structures made from softened dried peas harden, making them firm enough for strength testing.

2. Children look for lattice-type structures and their diagonal braces in the surrounding community—cranes, bridges, scaffolds, skyscraper skeletons, transmission towers, and so on. They record what they find in drawings and photos.

Related Reading

Jennings, Terry. *Structures*. Chicago: Children's Press, 1989.

Macaulay, David. *Castle*. Boston: Houghton Mifflin Co., 1977.

Macaulay, David. *Cathedral*. Boston: Houghton Mifflin Co., 1973.

Macaulay, David. *City*. Boston: Houghton Mifflin Co., 1974.

National Geographic Society. *Builders of the Ancient World*. Washington, DC: Author, 1986.

Weiss, Harvey. *What Holds It Together*. Boston: Little, Brown & Co., 1977.

Grades 2–3

Fasteners Used in Construction

Investigating and comparing how wood fasteners work

Key Experiences

- Testing: assessing properties by comparing effects of standardized procedures
- Measuring properties and changes using standard or nonstandard whole units

Materials

Six-inch strips of Styrofoam, or balsa wood, about 3⁄8-in. thick and 1-in. wide—enough for each pair of children to build simple bridges like the one shown; nails, wood screws, and nuts and bolts of adequate size to fasten the strips together; for each pair of children, a screwdriver, a hand drill, and a magnifying glass; small uniform objects to use as weights (e.g., washers)

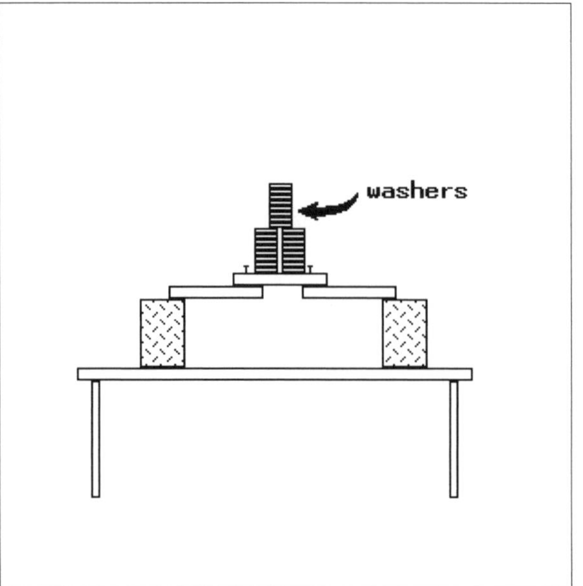

Activity

Children build simple bridges using the three different kinds of fasteners and then collect data on how much weight the bridges will bear before breaking down. The choice of soft building materials—balsa and Styrofoam—should minimize difficulties with inserting the nails, screws, or bolts and minimize the loads needed for testing the bridges. With the magnifying glass, children can look more closely at how screws are constructed, so they can compare them with the nails and bolts.

Two of the wood fasteners used in this activity—screws and nails—hold objects together by friction. The screw has the greater holding power partly because of the extensive surface area (on its thread) and partly because of the way its twisted blade cuts into and grips the object. The bolt and nut, on the other hand, encase the objects being joined.

Questions to Ask

How are the three kinds of fasteners alike? How are they different? How do you think that a nail holds two pieces together? How does a screw hold them? How does a bolt hold them? Does the thread on the bolt do the same job as the thread on the screw? Which fastener holds the bridge together best? For what kinds of fastening jobs would you use a nail? A screw? A bolt?

Extension

1. Children tour the school building and grounds to find places where nails, screws, and bolts are used. They make a chart recording their findings.

2. Using scrap lumber, children build other structures with nails, screws, and bolts. They build a tower, for example, and as they do so, choose the most effective fasteners for different holding tasks.

Related Reading

Iger, Martin, & Iger, Eve Marie. *Building a Skyscraper.* New York: Young Scott Books, 1967.

Macaulay, David. *City*. Boston: Houghton Mifflin Co., 1974.

Macaulay, David. *The Way Things Work*. Boston: Houghton Mifflin Co., 1988.

Grades 2–3

Testing Wood Fasteners

Investigating the holding power of fasteners of various forms

Key Experiences

- Testing: assessing properties by comparing effects of standardized procedures
- Ordering objects according to variation along a single dimension
- Using bar graphs

Materials

For each pair of children, two squares of 1-in.-thick Styrofoam; nails (6 penny–60 penny) and 1½ in.-long wood screws (4#–12#); a 1-gallon plastic bag or small pail and a wire twist fastener for attaching it to the screw or nail head; a set of uniform objects to use as weights (medium to large blocks)

Activity

After ordering the nails by thickness and the screws by thickness, children test the holding power of each fastener by seeing how many weights it will support when the weights are hung from the fastener as shown. After adding weights to the pail or plastic bag, one at a time, until each nail or screw pulls out of the Styrofoam, children can record and graph data for the various sizes of fasteners and thus draw conclusions about their relative effectiveness.

Generally, thicker screws or nails hold better than thinner ones do because, having more surface in contact with the board, they produce more friction. Usually, depth of penetration of the screw or nail is also an important factor in holding power, but in this case, since all the nails and screws are long enough to completely penetrate the object, this factor can be kept constant.

Questions to Ask

How does the screw grip the wood? How does the nail grip the wood? Why do they grip with different strengths? How does the thickness of the shank of the screw or nail affect its gripping power? What are some advantages of using screws instead of nails? Of using nails instead of screws?

Extension

Children use some nails that are alike except for their differing lengths, order them according to length, and test their holding power to see how important a nail's length is. (Of course, the object they drive the nails into must be at least as thick as the longest nail.)

Related Reading

Bramwell, Martyn, & Mostyn, David. *How Things Work*. London: Usborne Publishing Limited, 1984.

Macaulay, David. *The Way Things Work*. Boston: Houghton Mifflin Co., 1988.

Scharff, Robert. *Homeowner's Guide to Fastening Anything*. Nashville, TN: Ideals Publishing Corp., 1982.

Weiss, Harvey. *What Holds It Together*. Boston: Little, Brown & Co., 1977.

Grades 2–3

Fasteners for Shutting and Opening

Investigating how fasteners connect objects yet allow limited movement

Materials

For each pair of children, a pine board, about 10 in. × 12 in., with a smaller rectangular piece cut out of it to form a "door," and one or more loose-pin hinges; various door and gate fasteners (such as a hook and eye, turnbuckle, hasp, sliding bolt)—enough so that each child can choose a fastener to work with; a hand drill (manual or battery-driven); screws and screw drivers (both Phillips and standard)

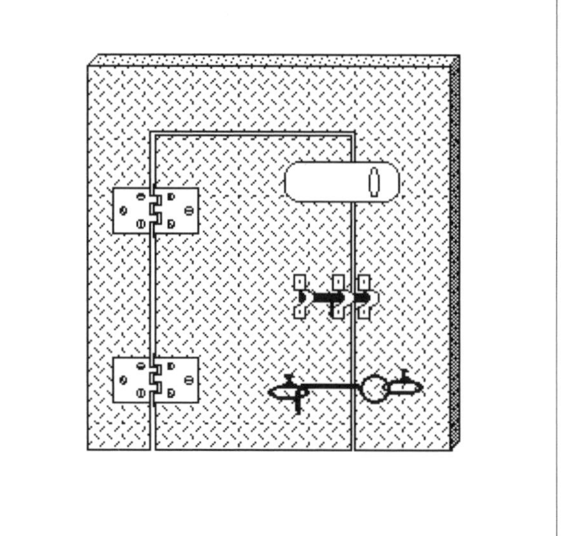

Activity

Children first screw the hinge(s) and then various fasteners to their "door," so they can compare how the fasteners work. Deciding where to drill the screw holes for the parts of each fastener will be a challenge and may require some trial and error.

Fasteners for doors, window, cabinets, and the like are frequently encountered and hence are of practical significance as structures for children to explore. By creating points of attachment, such fasteners restrict the movement of objects and keep them from coming apart. Unlike screws, nails, staples, or glue, however, the fasteners in this activity allow the fastened objects to have limited movement. Understanding how fasteners both restrict and allow movement is a lesson in causality.

You may want to introduce the technical terms for the various fasteners, but first encourage children to make up their own names for them.

Key Experiences

- Building structures with moving parts
- Improving a structure through trial-and-error modifications

Questions to Ask

Which fasteners are easy (or hard) to open? Easy (or hard) to close? How does your fastener keep the door from opening? Which fasteners were easy (or hard) to install? What problems did you have to solve in installing them?

Extension

1. Children disassemble old door knobs and key locks to investigate how they work.

2. Children visit a hardware or building supply store to see and try various types of fasteners, or they tour the school environment to find examples of gate and door and cabinet fasteners.

Related Reading

Bramwell, Martyn, & Mostyn, David. *How Things Work.* London: Usborne Publishing Limited, 1984

Cobb, Vicki. *The Secret Life of Hardware.* New York: Lippincott, 1982.

Macaulay, David. *The Way Things Work.* Boston: Houghton Mifflin Co., 1988.

Grades 2–3

Testing Glues

Testing glues as fasteners

Key Experiences

- Testing: assessing properties by comparing effects of standardized procedures
- Beginning to recognize that explaining a change may require keeping some variables (possible causes) constant

Materials

For each pair of children, a bathroom scale and a triangular block of wood: 6-in. strips of wood, at least ½-in. thick and about 2-in. wide, all of the same kind (pine, for example)—enough for each pair of children to test several kinds of glue; assorted glues (e.g., white craft glue, wood glue, model glue, white paste, wallpaper paste, mucilage)

Activity

Children use each of the various glues to glue a pair of wood strips together, overlapping each pair just 1 in. to keep the glued area the same in each case. Securing each joint with a rubber band and letting it sit overnight should allow the glues to dry. Then children can test each glued joint by positioning it on the triangular block, as shown, and seeing how many pounds of pressure are needed to break the joint. The data can be recorded and compared.

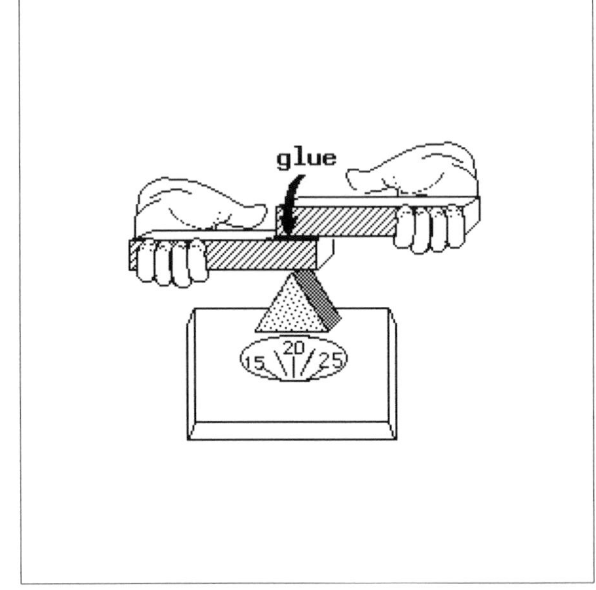

To keep the comparisons fair, several variables need to be "controlled"—the size of the test strips, the type of wood involved (i.e., the porosity of the glued surfaces), the surface area of the glued joint, and so on. This idea of what makes a test fair is something that children can begin to discuss and understand, but they will need some intervention from you in this area.

Questions to Ask

Which glues held best? Why is it important to keep the overlap of the strips the same in each glue test? What else might affect the strength of the glue joint? When would glue be a good fastener to use to attach two pieces of wood? When would glue not be a good fastener? Why might you fasten something, at the same time, with two kinds of fasteners—glue and a nail (or screw), for example?

Extension

1. Children try actually constructing something with scrap lumber and a good wood glue, learning to use clamps to hold glued joints while they dry.

2. Children test a single glue after they have allowed various drying times, or on surfaces with varying smoothness, to see how these alter the glue's effectiveness.

Related Reading

Lasson, Robert, & Shupak, Sidney. *Glue It Yourself.* New York: E. P. Dutton. 1977.

Macaulay, David. *The Way Things Work.* Boston: Houghton Mifflin Co., 1988.

Torre, Frank D. *Woodworking for Kids.* Garden City, NY: Doubleday & Co., Inc., 1978.

Grades 2–3

Bridges and Loads

Relating bridge design to load capacity

Key Experiences

- Improving a structure through trial-and-error modifications
- Testing: assessing properties by comparing effects of standardized procedures
- Identifying more than one factor affecting the operation or effectiveness of a structure

Materials

For each pair of children: two large blocks, bricks, or books of the same size; several 4-in. × 4-in. squares of paper of varying degrees of stiffness; a collection of uniform small objects (coins, washers, cubes) to use for weights

Activity

Children place the two large blocks a set distance apart (e.g., about 3 in.) and bridge the gap between them with a strip of paper. They try doing this first with a single strip and then with a single strip reinforced with a curved strip, trying both tests with all the different types of paper. To test each bridge, they try different loads (coins, washers, or cubes), adding more and more weights, one at a time, until the bridge collapses. (Keeping the strip centered over the gap and the load centered on the bridge is recommended.) They record their findings for each bridge design.

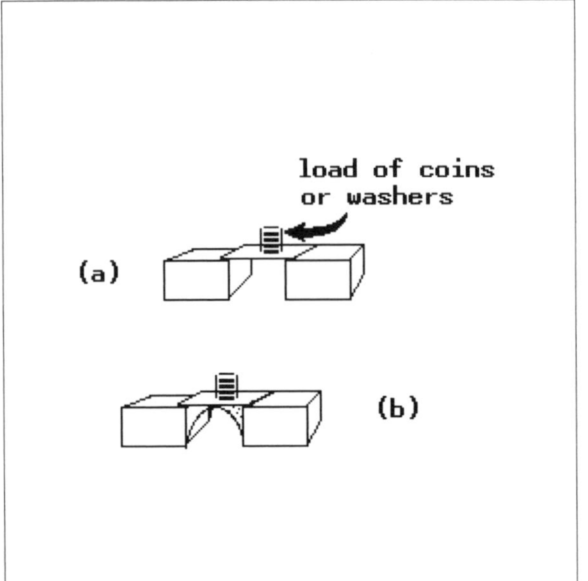

Keeping the two blocks a set distance apart and using just a strip of paper as the bridging material helps children focus attention on the importance of the nature and shape of the bridging material. The challenge in bridge design is often to find the minimum of materials needed to give the bridge strength to support a given load, whether it be a box of weights, a stream of pedestrians, or multiple lanes of bump-to-bumper traffic. Bridge building has been an engineering challenge throughout the ages.

Questions to Ask

How does using different kinds of paper affect the load that your bridge will hold? Which paper holds the smallest load? The greatest load? How are they different? When you bend a strip of paper into a curve, what happens to its ability to hold a load? Why do you think this is so? Can you think of any other way to bend or fold a strip of paper to change its ability to hold a load?

Extension

1. Children collect and display pictures of bridges. They build paper models of the bridges.

2. Children test one bridge design—perhaps just the flat-strip design—with different-sized gaps between the two supports, recording test results for the different-sized gaps.

Related Reading

Carlisle, Norman & Madelyn. *Bridges* (True Book Series). Chicago: Children's Press, 1965.

Coldwater, Daniel. *Bridges and How They Are Built.* New York: Young Scott Books, 1965.

Corbett, Scott. *Bridges.* New York: Four Winds Press, 1978.

Fogg, Christopher. *How They Built Long Ago.* New York: Warwick Press, 1981.

Pelta, Kathy. *Bridging the Golden Gate.* Minneapolis, MN: Lerner Publications, 1987.

Salvadori, Mario. *Building: The Fight Against Gravity.* New York: Atheneum, 1979.

Grade 3

Designing Girders

Designing and building girders and testing their load-bearing ability

Materials

For each pair of children: half sheets of typing paper, cut lengthwise (1⁄4 in. × 11 in.); tape; a small box, jar lid, or 3-in. × 3-in. square of heavy cardboard to hold weights; two bricks or large blocks of equal size; coins or washers for loading

Key Experiences

- Comparing the performance of similar structures
- Identifying more than one factor affecting the operation or effectiveness of a structure
- Testing: assessing properties by comparing effects of standardized procedures

Activity

Children design and build girders from the paper by rolling it into tubes or by folding it into triangular or other shapes. Then they use two girders of each design to bridge a gap between the bricks (or blocks). Keeping the gap between the books the same for each bridge they build, they use weights to test the load-bearing capacity for various girder designs, trying to build the girder that holds the most weight. They chart or graph the results and determine a shape that seems to work the best.

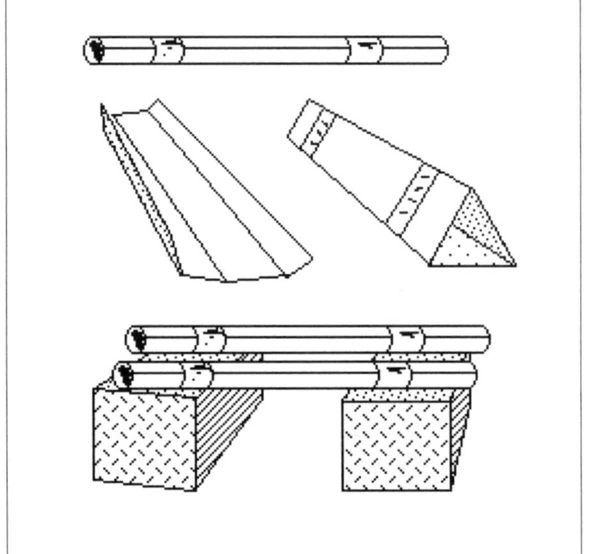

Beams and girders give strength to things like walls, ceilings, fences, bridges. A flat sheet of paper is quite flexible, but its rigidity can be greatly increased by rolling it into a tube or creasing it to form a triangular tube (for example, by twice folding the paper in half lengthwise and then overlapping two of the sections, as in the drawing). The strength of the girder is related to the size of its cross-section (a girder with a larger cross-section is generally stronger). The amount of overlap when the paper is folded or rolled also affects the strength of the girder. The distribution of the weight on the girder is another factor that influences how much weight it will hold.

Questions to Ask

What shapes were the girders you made? How did changing the shape of a girder affect its ability to support a load? What girder design held the most weight? Why do you think some shapes make a stronger girder than others?

Extension

Children look for beams and girders in structures around the school or around the community and try to decide where the load is on the girder—whether it is all on one part of the girder, on the middle of the girder, all along the girder, and so on. They also collect pictures of beams or girders.

Related Readings

Coldwater, Daniel. *Bridges and How They Are Built.* New York: Young Scott Books, 1965.

Corbett, Scott. *Bridges*. New York: Four Winds Press, 1978.

Salvadori, Mario. *Building: The Fight Against Gravity.* New York: Atheneum, 1979.

Grades 2–3

Sand Clocks

Constructing and using a sand timer

Key Experiences

- Using plans supplied by others to make more complex and functional structures
- Measuring properties and changes using standard or nonstandard whole units

Materials

For each pair of children: two plastic soda bottles; fine dry sand (screened beach sand or sandbox sand; avoid salt or sugar)—enough to fill about ¾ of a bottle; several small circles of cardboard the same size as the bottlenecks; scissors; strong tape; two equal strips of paper with regular units marked on them (to use as scales on the sides of the bottles); tool for punching very fine, clean holes in the cardboard circles (e.g., leather punch; drill; or hammer, thin nails, and wood block)

Activity

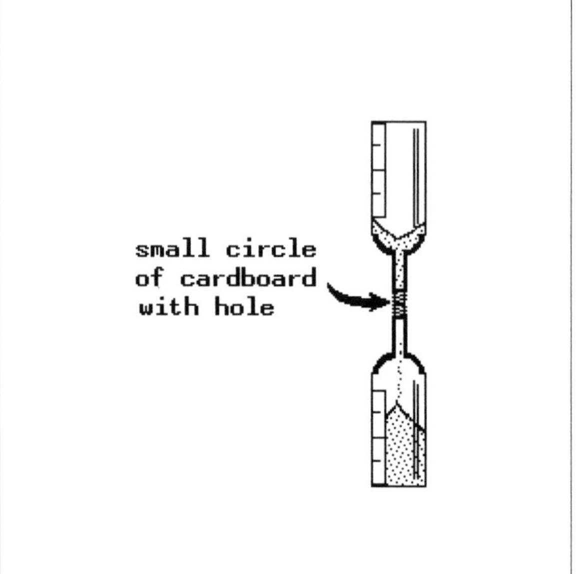

Children make a sand clock by taping the two soda bottles together at the neck, as shown. The small circle of cardboard between the bottle necks should have a clean, clear hole punched in it, to allow sand to flow slowly, but freely and steadily. Children can determine the best size of the hole by trial and error. (Though the children's timers may measure only short time intervals, with fine-enough sand, a fine-enough hole, and large soft drink bottles, a timer can be made to measure up to a ½-hour interval.)

After constructing a sand clock that works as they want it to, children can take turns timing each other doing short tasks (e.g., solving a puzzle, covering an obstacle course). To make the sand clock permanent and stable, they can tape dowels or wood strips to its sides.

Questions to Ask

Which sand timers flow faster? Which flow slower? Why do some timers flow faster than others? What kinds of things did you time with your timer? Would your timer tell you when it was time to wake up or time to go to school? How is it different from modern clocks? How is it the same?

Extension

1. Children use different scales on their sand timers (strips marked in finer or larger intervals, for example) and see how this makes a difference in how they can use their timer. They also relate the marks on their sand timer's scale to the minutes on a conventional clock.

2. Children integrate their learning about time measurement with social studies themes, discussing, for example, attitudes about time or methods of time measurement in cultures they are studying.

Related Reading

Bendick, Jeanne. *The First Book of Time* (pp. 43–44). New York: Franklin Watts, Inc., 1963.

Buehr, Walter. *Keeping Time* (pp. 34–38). New York: G. P. Putnam's Sons, 1960.

Catherall, Ed. *Clocks and Time* ("Making a Sand Clock," p. 11). Hove, East Sussex, England: Wayland Publishers Limited, 1982.

Tannenbaum, Beulah, & Stillman, Myra. *Understanding Time* (pp. 43–44). New York: McGraw-Hill Book Co., Inc., 1958.

Tarner, Anthony. *Time Museum Catalogue of the Collection, Vol. I: Time Measuring Instruments.* Rockford, IL: Time Museum, 1984.

Grades 1–2

A Sun Clock

Observing changes in shadows cast by the sun

Key Experiences

- Using plans supplied by others to make more complex and functional structures
- Observing changes over time
- Measuring properties and changes using standard or nonstandard whole units

Materials

For each pair of children: a pencil or dowel, 3-in.–4-in. long; a flat board, about 1 ft × 1 ft, with a hole drilled in the center for the pencil or dowel (or a stiff paper plate and a lump of clay to hold the pencil or dowel)

Activity

Children construct a sundial as shown. They place it in a spot that has full sun all day and record the position of the pencil's (or dowel's) shadow at various times of the day.

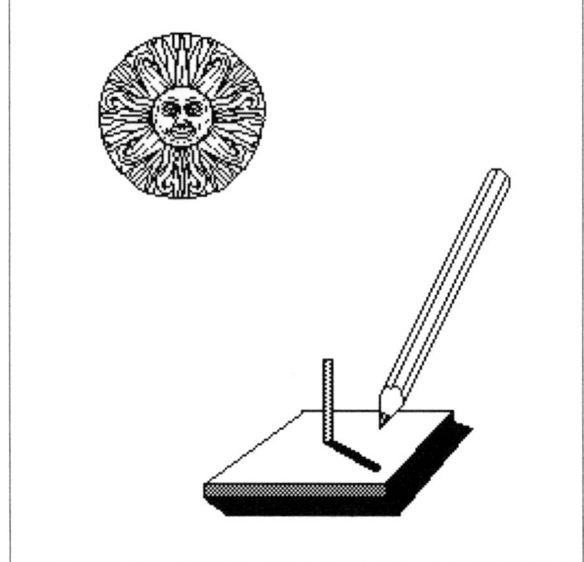

The sundial is a very old timing instrument used by ancient Greeks and Romans. The positions of the shadows repeat from one day to the next as the sun "moves" (appears to us to be in different positions) across the sky. If one notes the position of the shadow at the beginning of lunch one day, for example, lunchtime the next day can be anticipated as the sun's shadow approaches the same place on the dial. Of course, the sundial must remain in the same location!

Actually, from season to season, the shadow positions will change because the sun appears higher and lower in the sky as the cycle of seasons progresses. These changes are small on a day-to-day basis, however, so they will not be noticed unless the sundial is observed (and left unmoved) over the course of many weeks. The Romans learned that by inclining the gnomon (the pencil or dowel) of the sundial so it pointed to the North Star, they could make the shadows fall in the same place each hour regardless of the time of year.

Questions to Ask

What causes the shadow? How does the shadow change over the day? Why do you think it changes? How could you use a sundial? When could you not use a sundial?

Extension

1. Children learn how early peoples used the sundial. They observe a sundial with both a vertical and an inclined gnomon, marking the positions of the shadows each hour of the day.

2. Children mark which shadow positions on the sundial coincide with the events in their daily schedule and mark the sundial accordingly to make a "daily schedule" clock.

Related Reading

Buehr, Walter. *Keeping Time* (pp. 34–36). New York: G. P. Putnam's Sons, 1960.

Catherall, Ed. *Clocks and Time* ("Shadows," pp. 5–8). Hove, East Sussex, England: Wayland Publishers Limited, 1982.

Kehoe, Rick, & Kehoe, Alma. *Clocks Tell the Time* (pp. 6–7, pp. 10–11). New York: Charles Scribner's Sons, 1960.

Tannenbaum, Beulah, & Stillman, Myra. *Understanding Time* ("Sun Clocks," pp. 16–32). New York: McGraw-Hill Book Co., Inc., 1958.

Tarner, Anthony. *Time Museum Catalogue of the Collection, Vol. I: Time Measuring Instruments.* Rockford, IL: Time Museum, 1984.

Grades 2–3

Weighing With an Elastic Band

Building a spring scale

Key Experiences

- Using plans supplied by others to make more complex and functional structures
- Measuring properties and changes using standard or nonstandard whole units

Materials

For each pair of children: a piece of 1⁄4-in . (or narrower) elastic, 18-in.–24-in. long; a yard stick or a thin board, about 36-in. long; string; thumb tacks; paper clip "hooks"; a set of uniform objects (e.g., coins, 3⁄8-in. washers) to use as weights; a plastic sandwich bag (to hold weights); a paper strip (for marking a scale that measures stretch of the elastic)

Activity

Children construct a spring scale as shown. Then they calibrate the scale by first marking a zero-point on the strip of paper (the place the mark on the elastic originally aligns with). Next, they add one weight at a time and mark the strip of paper to show how much farther each additional weight stretches the elastic. Finally, they use their spring scale to weigh different small objects (in nonstandard units, of course) and to compare the weights of different small objects (e.g., scissors, glue bottle, medium block, small toy, apple).

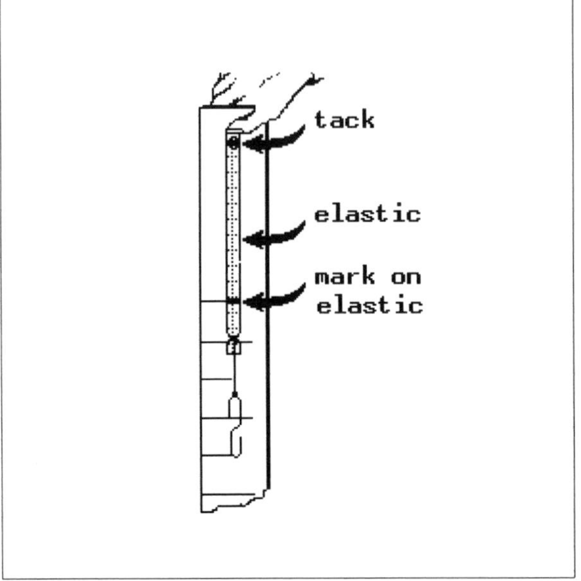

The children's spring scale will be calibrated in nonstandard units, so they will be able to weigh objects to see how many blocks, nails, or washers each is equivalent to. However, when it is calibrated using standard weights, such as 10-gram weights, a spring scale allows weights and other forces to be measured in standard units without having a set of standard weights on hand (as is required with a balance scale). In addition, the spring scale is useful for measuring such forces as the pull of a parachute, or the pull on a kite string or rope.

Questions to Ask

How did you construct your spring scale? What are some things you can weigh with your scale? How can you use your spring scale to decide which is the heavier of two objects? What are some things too small to weigh with your scale? Too large to weigh with your scale? How could you make a spring scale to weigh smaller (larger) objects?

Extension

1. Children try using different widths of elastic and see how this changes the calibrations on the scale and the kinds of things they can weigh.

2. Children try using a spring scale to measure a pulling force on a string. They place the scale flat on a table, for example, and tie a small battery-powered or wind-up toy to the hook on the elastic. Adding a screw eye at the top and bottom of the elastic helps to keep it in line with the ruler.

Related Reading

Pine, Tillie, & Levine, Joseph. *Measurements, And How We Use Them.* New York: McGraw-Hill Book Co., Inc., 1977.

Russell, Solveig P. *Size, Distance, Weight.* New York: Henry Z. Walck, Inc., 1968.

Srivastova, Jane. *Weighing and Balancing.* New York: Thomas Y. Crowell Co., 1970.

Grades 2–3

Simple Circuits

Discovering how to design a circuit to light a bulb

Key Experiences

- Building with simple electrical circuits
- Using models, drawings, and diagrams to illustrate oral or written reports

Materials

For each pair of children: a flashlight battery (C or D—rechargeable, if possible); a 2-cell flashlight bulb; lengths of thin (#22) insulated wire (with plastic insulation removed from the ends)

Activity

Children explore a battery, a bulb, and some wires, in an effort to make the bulb light up. They make drawings of their successful and unsuccessful circuit designs.

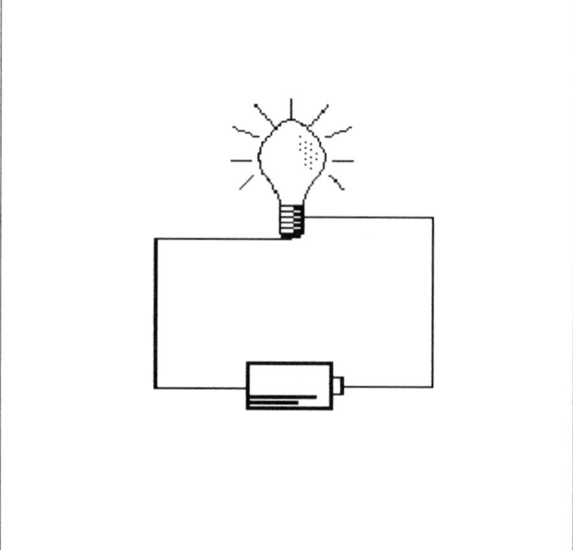

While the ultimate mechanisms of electrical forces and energy may be difficult for children to probe, they can nevertheless come to appreciate the structure of a circuit by exploring the interaction of components like batteries, bulbs, and switches. They can discover, for example, that the battery and the bulb must be parts of a loop formed by two wires (as shown), with the wires connecting the two contacts on the battery with the two contacts on the bulb (the bulb's contact points are on the base and on the side of the bulb). Though the light can be switched off by breaking this loop at any point, initially children will most likely think of breaking the loop at one of the contact points.

Questions to Ask

What did you do to make the lightbulb come on? How can you make it go off and then on again? Is there more than one way to do this? How many wires did you use to make your circuit? Can you light the bulb using only two wires? Can it be done with only one wire? How did you attach your wires to the contact points? Can you think of any other ways to attach them?

Extension

1. Children devise ways to securely attach wires to bulbs and batteries. These can be improvised using spring clothespins, corks, coiled wire and tape, rubber bands, and so on.

2. Once the wires are securely attached at the contact points, children use a piece of wood or cardboard, paper clips, tape, tacks, and brass fasteners to build a switch that makes it easy to make and break the loop at a point other than the four contact points.

3. Children try using two bulbs at the same time in a circuit. They use this idea to devise a battery light system for a doll house or a diorama.

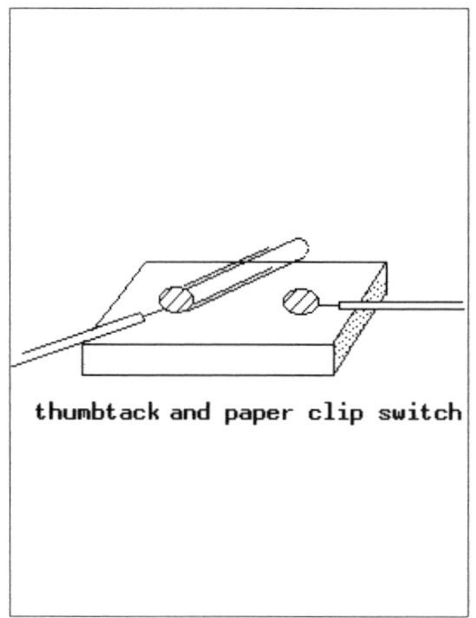

Devising switches with paper clips, tape, tacks, brass fasteners, and other everyday materials is another way children can apply their developing understanding of circuits.

Related Reading

Bains, Rae. *Discovering Electricity.* Mahwah, NJ: Troll Associates, 1982.

Berger, Melvin. *Switch On, Switch Off.* New York: Harper Collins Publishers, 1989.

Catherall, Ed. *Electric Power.* Hove, East Sussex, England: Wayland Publishers Limited, 1981.

Epstein, Sam & Epstein, Beryl. *Electricity.* New York: Franklin Watts, Inc., 1977.

Marble, Sandra. *Power Up: Experiments, Puzzles, & Games Exploring Electricity.* New York: Macmillan, 1989.

Rosenfield, Sam. *The Magic of Electricity.* New York: Lothrop, Lee and Shepard, Inc., 1963.

Ward, Alan. *Experimenting With Batteries, Bulbs, & Wires.* North Pomfet, VT: Trafalgar Square, 1986.

9
▼
Energy and Change

Grades 1–2

Force—A Push or a Pull

Experiencing force as a push or a pull that produces change

Key Experiences

- Manipulating physical objects to produce an effect or change
- Relating the magnitude of an effect to the magnitude of a cause
- Identifying more than one possible cause for a change

Materials

A sturdy carton, large enough for a child to sit in; a 1-ft piece of clothesline; a bathroom scale; 10 cylindrical rods of equal size (e.g., pieces of broom handle or dowel rods)—to use as rollers under the box

Activity

(Suitable for a large group)

Children experience "force" as a push by having various volunteers sit in the carton and trying to push the carton ("loaded" with one child) across a smooth floor. Then, holding a bathroom scale against the side of the carton and pushing on the scale, they determine how many pounds of force it takes to set the loaded carton in motion. Children can also weigh themselves on the bathroom scale, to compare their own poundage to the poundage needed to move the carton with them in it. They can also try the same pushing activities after putting rollers under the carton (which should enable it to move more easily).

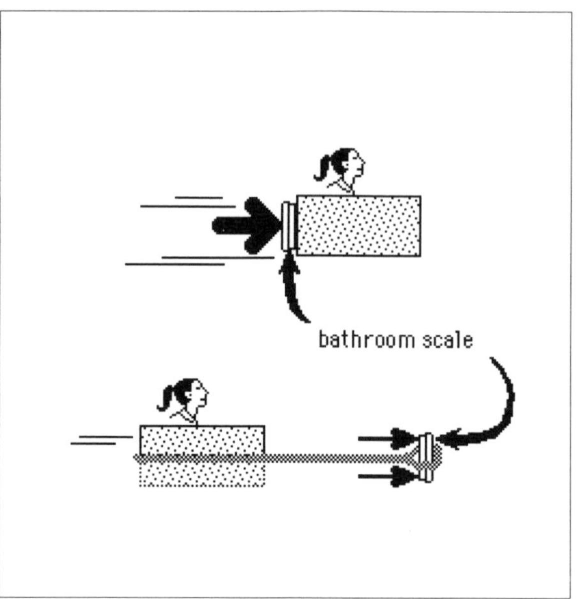

To experience force as a pull, they can tie one end of the rope around the carton and the other end around the scale. Then, holding the scale vertically with fingertips pressing on the bottom of the scale, they can try pulling the loaded carton while someone reads the scale to see how many pounds of pulling are needed to start the carton moving. (Keeping the rope as close to horizontal as possible is recommended.)

In this activity, children experience force directly as the force exerted by their muscles in moving an object. In later activities, they will discover forces being produced in other ways—by rolling and falling balls, by wind, by falling water. Using a bathroom scale to measure the pushing and pulling force exerted in this activity is not as far-fetched as it may seem. What do we measure, after all, when we determine our weight on a bathroom scale? The force (called gravity) attracting us toward the earth!

Questions to Ask

How many pounds of force did you use to push (pull) the loaded carton? Did the push (pull) you needed change when different people sat in the box? Is the force required to push a load the same as that required to pull it? When you stand on a scale, what force are you measuring? How did using the rollers under the carton change the force needed to move it? What else could change the amount of force you need to move it? Do you think the force you used to move the loaded carton is the same as the weight of the loaded carton? How does the force used to move the loaded carton compare to its weight? How can you record your findings about all of this?

Extension

Children measure the push or pull needed to move the carton on various kinds of surfaces—the gym floor, a tile floor, the sidewalk, asphalt, smooth carpeting—and make a graph showing the kinds of surfaces and the pounds of pushing or pulling force each required. On the basis of what they see in this graph, they try to predict how easily the loaded carton would move on some other surfaces—ice, shag carpet, foam padding.

Related Readings

Ardley, Neil. *Force and Strength.* New York: Franklin Watts, 1985.

Arvetis, Chris. *What Is Gravity?* Middletown, CT: Field Publications, 1986.

Cobb, Vicki. *Why Doesn't the Earth Fall Up?* New York: Lodestar Books, E. P. Dutton, 1988.

Laithwaite, Eric. *Force: The Power Behind Movement.* New York: Franklin Watts, 1986.

Walpole, Brenda. *Movement* (pp. 2–6, 16–22). New York: Warwick Press, 1987.

Grades 2–3

Exploring Forces

Comparing and measuring forces with a "spring scale"

Materials

For each pair of children: several books of equal size and weight; an 18-in.–24-in. strip of 1/4-in. elastic knotted at one end (to keep it from slipping out of the book); a measuring stick marked in units (standard or nonstandard)

Key Experiences

- Increasing or decreasing a causal factor and comparing the effects produced
- Measuring properties and changes using standard or nonstandard whole units

Activity

Children insert the elastic between the pages of one book and pull on the other end of the elastic strip, while the book is lying on a smooth surface, to see when the book begins to move. They devise a way to place the measuring stick to measure how far the piece of elastic must stretch before the book will budge. They then add a second book on top of the first and repeat. They add additional books and try again, recording and graphing the results.

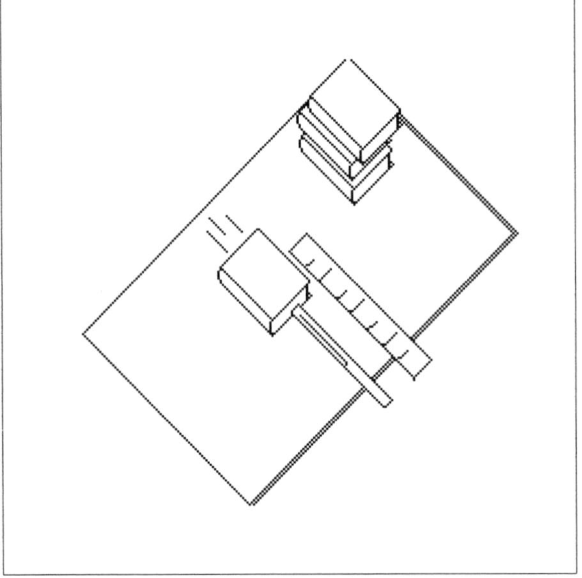

In this activity, instead of measuring the required force in pounds, children measure it in units of length—a crude "spring scale" measurement. They might, in this activity, begin to think about the force that is resisting their pull on the elastic, which is the frictional force between the book and the table. This force is proportional (but not necessarily equal) to the weight of the book. It depends on both the smoothness of the surfaces interfacing (the table's and the book's) and the weight of the book. This means that for a particular pair of book and table surfaces, the force of friction is greater for a heavier book than for a lighter book. For example, if the book weight is doubled, the pull needed to overcome friction is doubled; if the book weight is tripled, the pull is tripled; and so on.

Questions to Ask

Did each book begin to move as soon as you pulled on the elastic? What force made a book begin to move across the table? How did you measure the force it took to begin to move the book? What do you think keeps some books from moving at first? If a book didn't move right away, how far did you have to stretch the elastic before the book began to move? What do you think would happen if you tried the same activity—pulling the same books with elastic—on a carpeted surface?

Extension

1. Children weigh the books, make a graph that shows the weight and the force needed to move each book, and look for a pattern.

2. Children try the same activity on different surfaces, using the same books and the same elastic strip.

Related Reading

Branley, Franklyn M. *Weight and Weightlessness.* New York: Thomas Y. Crowell Co., 1971.

Selsam, Millicent E. *Up, Down, and Around.* Garden City, NY: Doubleday & Co., Inc., 1977.

Simon, Seymour. *Motion.* New York: Coward-McCann, Inc., 1968.

Walpole, Brenda. *Movement* (pp. 4–6, 12–16, 30). New York: Warwick Press, 1987.

Webster, Vera R. *Science Experiments* (pp. 5–20, 32). Chicago: Children's Press, 1982.

Grade K

Bouncing Balls

Relating properties of materials to their ability to store energy

Materials

For each pair of children: a collection of soft and hard, large and small balls—tennis ball, golf ball, ping-pong ball, Wiffle ball, racquet ball, beach ball, baseball, Nerf ball, yarn ball, billiard ball

Activity

Children informally test the various balls by trying to bounce them on a hard surface (such as a tile or wood floor). They observe properties of the balls (whether they are soft, hard, big, small, squishy, heavy, light) and decide if these relate to their bounciness.

Experience with bouncing balls can introduce children to the concept of energy. For a ball to bounce, the energy of motion of the moving ball must be stored in the ball or the floor (by compression) and then returned to the ball as it resumes its motion, now in a different direction, back up. If a ball or the surface it hits is not resilient, the ball doesn't bounce well because much of its energy of motion is taken up in changing the shape of the ball or the floor (e.g, as with a carpet that is pressed down by the ball.) Thus, soft, malleable balls (or surfaces) produce the least bounce.

Children, of course, are not expected to come up with this detailed explanation of the energy concept but rather to observe what they can about the features of balls that bounce well.

Questions to Ask

Which balls bounce well? Which don't bounce well? What differences do you see between the balls that bounce well and those that don't? Why do you think some balls bounce better than others?

Key Experiences

- Repeating an activity that produces a change to gain awareness of possible causes
- Identifying more than one possible cause for a change

Extension

1. Children try bouncing an inflatable ball when it is inflated to different degrees and compare how it bounces with different amounts of inflation.

2. Children try bouncing one particular ball on a variety of surfaces (sand, asphalt, carpet, concrete, foam padding) to see how this affects its bounciness. The denting of the surface is easy to see in some of these cases.

3. Children compare the bounce of each of a variety of rubber balls, so that such qualities as hardness, hollowness, or size are the only differences they can observe.

4. Using various-sized ball bearings and a steel surface, children investigate how they bounce on such a surface and then how they bounce on another hard, but nonsteel, surface.

Related Reading

Cobb, Vicki. *Why Doesn't the Earth Fall Up?* New York: Lodestar Books, 1988.

Satchwell, John. *Energy at Work* (p. 16). New York: Lothtrop, Lee & Shepard Books, 1981.

Tafuri, Nancy. *The Ball Bounced.* New York: Greenwillow Books, 1989.

Grades 1–3

Measuring Bounce

Discovering that the height of a ball's bounce is a measure of its ability to store energy

Key Experiences

- Measuring properties and changes using standard or nonstandard whole units
- Testing: assessing properties by comparing effects of standardized procedures
- Using bar graphs

Materials

A collection of balls like those used for the previous activity.

Activity

Children roll each ball off the edge of a table, mark or measure the height of the ball's first bounce, and graph the various bounce heights. Teacher introduces the concepts of "energy of motion" and "stored energy."

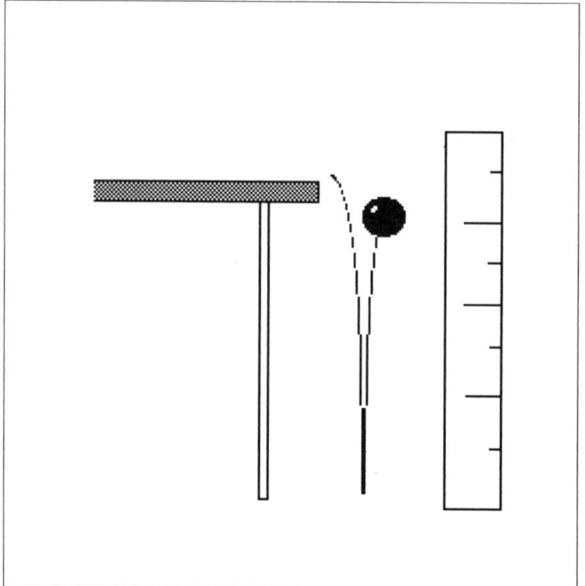

Though we cannot view energy directly, we can view the effects of energy transfers. For example, hurricanes and lightning produce effects, sometimes devastating ones, because of their tremendous energy. Moving balls have energy too. Balls rolled off a table gain "energy of motion" as they fall and pick up speed. As they hit the floor, some of their energy of motion is transferred to stored energy by compression. This stored energy is again changed to energy of motion as the ball bounces back, but some is lost, which explains why balls don't bounce the full height of their fall. (Some energy is lost as the ball and the floor flex as the ball hits and changes its direction; also, on impact, some energy is changed into sound and heat energy). The higher the ball bounces after falling from the table, the better it is at storing its energy of motion.

Questions to Ask

How high did each ball bounce after rolling off the table? Why do you think some balls bounce higher than others?

Extension

Children order the balls in this activity according to hardness (they squeeze or poke them with a sharp object to determine this). Then they compare the "hardness ranking" of a ball with its "bounce-height ranking." Seeing some relationship between hardness and bounce, they try to use hardness to predict the bounce of some new balls that you introduce.

Related Reading

Satchwell, John. *Energy at Work* (p. 16). New York: Lothrop, Lee & Shepard Books, 1981.

Tafuri, Nancy. *The Ball Bounced.* New York: Greenwillow Books, 1989.

White Laurence B. *Science Tricks* ("Making an Egg That Bounces"). Reading, MA: Addison-Wesley Publishing Co., 1975.

Grades K--1

Rolling Balls

Experiencing rolling motion as a form of energy that can produce change

Key Experiences

- Observing and describing a pattern of change
- Comparing the performance of similar materials

Materials

For each pair of children: a collection of balls of various weights—baseball, tennis ball, croquet ball, softball, golf ball, Wiffle ball, yarn ball; a 3-ft–4-ft board wide enough to use as a ramp for the balls (or a length of eaves trough); several identical blocks to support the ramp at various heights; a block to set at the end of the ramp as a "target"

Activity

Children explore the various kinds of balls and get the feel of rolling them down a ramp toward a target block (some trial and error may be involved in deciding on a ramp height and getting the balls to hit the target block). Then they roll each ball down the ramp to see how far it moves the target block (perhaps marking the block's stopping point each time).

You may find that the balls will roll more directly toward the target if the ramp has some sort of side rails or if a "V"-shaped ramp is used.

In this activity, children explore the speed and power in movement. Although we cannot see energy directly, we are aware of the effects of energy transfer—movement of the target block. Balls of different size, weight, and speed (which is increased by raising the ramp) have different degrees of impact on the block. The greater the impact, the more energy the rolling balls have imparted to the target block.

Questions to Ask

Are there any differences in how the balls roll? Which balls move the block the farthest? Why do you think some balls move the block farther than others? How does this relate to your other experiments with balls?

Extension

1. Using the same balls and target, children experiment with different ramp heights to see how this affects the impact on the target. They record the results in a chart.

2. Children experiment with different ramp lengths—that is, with rolling each ball from specific marked points on the same ramp—to see how ramp length relates to impact.

3. This same activity is tried on the playground, rolling the assorted balls down a slide and having someone catch each ball at the end of the slide to feel the difference in impact of different balls. The role of ramp length is investigated by using various starting points for rolling the balls.

Related Reading

Kerrod, Robin. *Science Alive, Moving Things* ("Force and Movement," pp. 22–23). Morristown, NJ: Silver Burdett Press, 1987.

Macaulay, David. *The Way Things Work*. Boston: Houghton Mifflin Co., 1988.

Onii, Eiji, & Onii, Masako. *Simple Science Experiments With Marbles*. Milwaukee, WI: Gareth Stevens, 1989.

Walpole, Brenda. *Movement, Fun With Science* (pp. 16–20). New York: Warwick Press, 1987.

Grades 1–3

Pendulum Clocks

Building pendulums of different lengths and observing how the pendulum's swing changes

Key Experiences

- Observing and describing a pattern of change
- Relating the magnitude of an effect to the magnitude of a cause

Materials

For each pair of children: a spool of string or thread, a large washer for a weight, a stick to suspend the pendulum from, some heavy weight to secure the stick to a table or other high surface

Activity

Children construct a pendulum clock by tying a string (or thread) to a stick, attaching the washer to the end of the string, and holding the stick in such a way that the string and its weight can swing freely. They count swings for the pendulum they have made, noting whether they have to count quickly or slowly to keep up with the pendulum (children will most likely count one arc, e.g., the weight going once from right to left, as "one swing"). Each pair of children can then use their pendulum to time some simple, short activity "in swings," such as how long it takes each of them to tie a bow, or put together a simple puzzle.

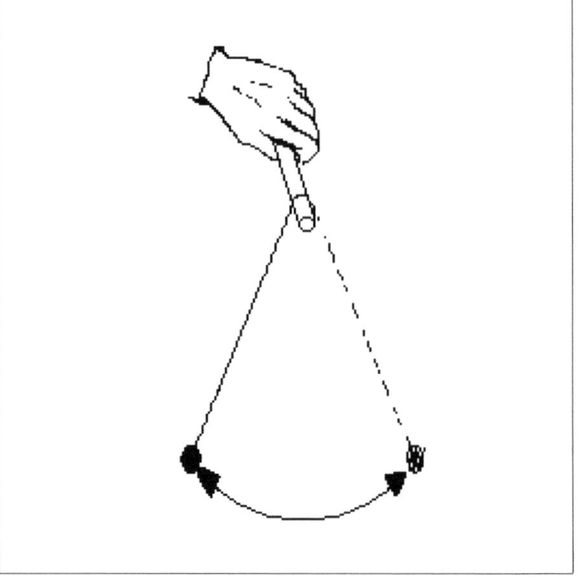

When children notice that other pairs of children have made pendulums that require quicker or slower counting, encourage them to try shortening and lengthening their pendulum's string to see what effect this has on how they must count the swings.

The pendulum's steady swing has been used as a timing device for centuries. Even its oldest users had discovered that what is called the pendulum's *period* (time to traverse *two* arcs, e.g., left to right and back again) depends only on the length of the pendulum. Differences in the weight at the end and in the width of the swing do not affect the period.

Since gravity is the force that makes the pendulum swing back and forth at a regular rate, where the pendulum is on the earth also has some effect on its period. For example, a pendulum swings more quickly at sea level than at the top of a mountain (where gravity is slightly weaker)—but this is not a difference children will be able to observe in classroom exploration. At sea level, a pendulum about 1 meter in length will swing (traverse 1 arc) every second. At one time, in fact, the length of a pendulum with a 1-second swing was proposed as the standard unit for the metric system.

Questions to Ask

When you first made your pendulum, how long was it? Did it swing slowly or quickly? What kinds of things did you time with your pendulum? How many swings did you count for your partner (doing some task)? For yourself? What happened when you tried shorter or longer pendulums? What do you think is a good length for a pendulum that you want to time (name some short or long task) with?

Extension

1. Children can use a 1-minute egg timer or a stopwatch to see how many swings their various pendulums make in a minute. They can make a graph showing pendulum length and number of swings.

2. Children can devise a way to make a very long pendulum, one that can hang from a ceiling, for example, and explore what kinds of events or tasks they can time with such a pendulum.

3. Children who understand minutes and seconds can use a stopwatch or an egg timer to try to find a length of pendulum that swings 60 times in a minute (i.e., once each second)

Related Reading

Bendick, Jeanne. *The First Book of Time* (p. 45). New York: Franklin Watts, Inc., 1963.

Catherall, Ed. Clocks and Time ("Mechanical Clocks," pp. 13–22). Hove, East Sussex, England: Wayland Publishers Limited, 1982.

Cobb, Vicki. *Why Doesn't the Earth Fall Up?* (pp. 37–38). New York: E. P. Dutton, 1988.

Tannenbaum, Beulah, & Stillman, Myra. *Understanding Time* (pp. 52–65). New York: McGraw-Hill Book Co., Inc., 1958.

Grades 2–3

A Spool Tractor

Experiencing how energy stored in a rubber band is released and produces movement

Key Experiences

- Building structures with moving parts
- Relating the magnitude of an effect to the magnitude of a cause

Materials

For each child, a large thread spool (foam spools are best); a rubber band, a thumb tack, a washer, and a pencil

Activity

By inspecting a model tractor, children see how to build spool tractors like the one pictured. After winding up their tractors by holding the spool fixed and turning the pencil, they explore what happens when the tractors are released on the floor.

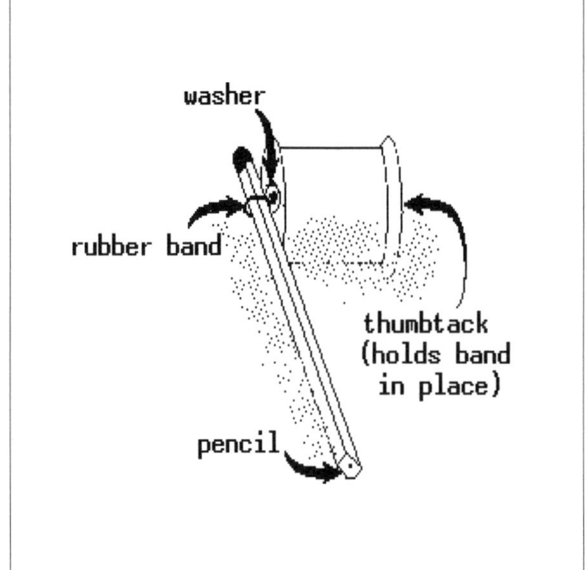

As happens with any manual wind-up toy, "human energy" is stored in the tractor's rubber band.when it is wound. The stored human energy is expended when the spool tractor is released and allowed to scoot across the floor. (The washer keeps the pencil from binding on the side of the spool.)

Children can explore the relationship between the number of turns they give the pencil and the distance the tractor goes. They might, for example, make a graph relating distance traveled with number of turns. They will find that a greater number of turns stores up more human energy, which can then be used to move the tractor a greater distance on the floor.

Questions to Ask

What happens to the rubber band when the pencil is wound around and around? Why does the wound-up tractor move when it is released? How can you make one tractor go farther than another?

1. Children can use the tractors to push or pull small loads (as in a real-life tractor pull) and explore

what factors determine how much a tractor will pull and how far it will pull a load. If they use small, uniform objects to make up the loads (small blocks, or large nails, for example) they might graph information about loads and numbers of wind-up turns.

2. Children can experiment with running their tractors up ramps to see which ones have enough energy to climb the ramp and how far they will climb for various numbers of turns. They might also experiment with providing better "traction" by outfitting the spools with rubber band "tires."

3. Children can make a giant-sized version of the spool tractor by using, instead of the spool, a cylindrical plastic squeeze bottle (like a shampoo bottle) with its cap perforated. An elastic band is run through the cap and bottle and secured at the bottom of the bottle.

Supplying children with the materials and challenging them to design such a tractor might be possible, once they have seen how the spool tractor works.

4. Children can discuss other ways they use human energy to cause motion—pedaling bicycles, pushing a skateboard or scooter, kicking a floatboard, paddling a boat, pumping their legs or pushing to make a swing move. Children discuss cultures in which human and animal energy are the primary ways motion is produced—this ties in well with social studies units on traditional cultures.

5. Children might take apart a commercially available wind-up toy and examine the energy-storing mechanism, comparing it to their spool tractor.

Related Reading

Kerrod, Robin. *Science Alive, Moving Things* ("Simple Machines" pp. 24–25). Morristown, NJ: Silver Burdett Press, 1987.

Macaulay, David. *The Way Things Work*. Boston: Houghton Mifflin Company, 1988.

Scarry, Huck. *On Wheels*. New York: The Putnam Publishing Group, 1980.

Zubrowski, Bernie. *Wheels at Work: Experimenting With Models of Machines*. New York: Morrow, 1986.

Grade 2

Motion Produced by Wind

Discovering that wind energy creates forces that can cause objects to move

Key Experiences

- Building structures with moving parts
- Identifying a cause for a change
- Comparing the performance of similar structures

Materials

For each pair of children: a pencil with an eraser; two straight pins and two small beads; a 6-in. × 6-in. square and a 3-in. × 3-in. square of construction paper or lightweight cardboard; scissors; and a fan or hair dryer

Activity

Children make two pinwheels, as shown, by cutting each square at the corners to form blades and then folding (to the square's center) one corner of each blade. A large pin, with a bead to reduce friction, fastens each pinwheel to a pencil. Children observe the motion of the pinwheels outdoors in both light and strong winds, if possible. They also test the pinwheels indoors with high and low fan (or hair dryer) settings.

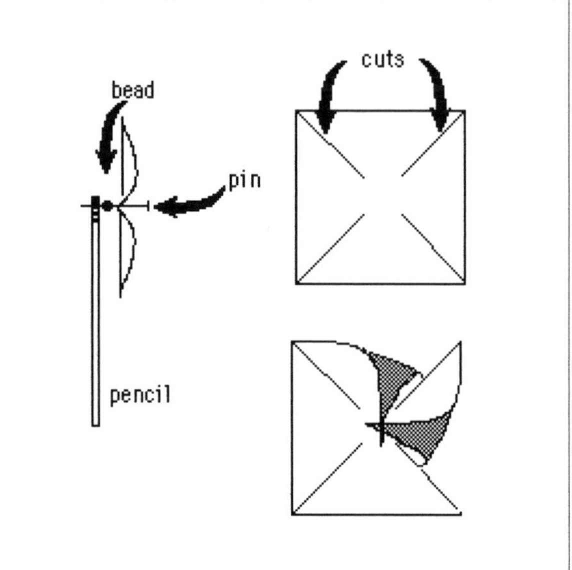

The energy of moving air—wind—has been used over the centuries to produce force to move such things as windmills and sailing ships. Experiencing the pinwheel's motion is a good way for children to see how wind energy can create a turning force. Compared to the small pinwheel, the large pinwheel catches more air and consequently produces more turning force for a given wind speed; however, it turns more slowly. The small pinwheel turns faster but without as much turning force, and in a light wind, it may fail to turn altogether (owing to friction with the pin and bead).

Questions to Ask

What makes the pinwheels move? What differences do you see in the way the large and small pinwheels turn? What might cause these differences? Does it make any difference whether you test the pinwheels indoors or outdoors? In a light or a strong wind? Can you think of ways to improve the way your windmills turn? Could you find a way to use the turning force of a pinwheel to do some work, like making a car go?

Extension

1. Children test other effects of moving air, for example, by fanning a feather with a hand fan, blowing through a drinking straw to move a ping pong ball, using a vacuum cleaner to pick up sawdust or sand.

2. In conjunction with a unit on a region in which wind power is a major source of energy, children read about windmills and try building a working model of a windmill.

3. Children make windsocks, kites, and flags and experiment with them in light and heavy winds, seeing how different materials and methods of construction affect how they work.

4. Children experiment with powering model boats with various sizes and shapes of homemade sails.

Related Reading

Catherall, Ed. *Wind Power.* Hove, East Sussex, England: Wayland Publishers Limited, 1981.

De Vinck, Antoine. *Wim of the Wind.* Garden City, NY: Doubleday & Co., 1974.

Dyson, John, & Dyson, Kate. *Fun With Kites.* Woodbury, NY: Barron's Educational Series, Inc. 1978.

Hutchins, Pat. *The Wind Blew.* New York: Macmillan Publishing Co., Inc., 1974.

Macaulay, David. *The Way Things Work.* Boston: Houghton Mifflin Co., 1988.

Marks, Burton, & Marks, Rita. *Kites for Kids.* New York: Lothrop, Lee & Shepard Books, 1980.

Newman, Jay Hartly, & Lee, Scott. *Kite Craft.* New York: Crown Publishers, Inc., 1974.

Watson, Jane Werner. *Alternate Energy Sources* ("Energy From Moving Air," pp. 30-41). New York: Franklin Watts, Inc., 1979.

Grade 3

Measuring Wind Force

Constructing an anemometer

Key Experiences

- Building structures with moving parts
- Relating the magnitude of an effect to the magnitude of a cause
- Measuring properties and changes using standard or nonstandard whole units

Materials

For each pair of children: a piece of stiff wire or wooden dowel about 15-in. long; three or four 2-in. × 5-in. strips of differing weights—e.g., one each of lightweight paper, heavy cardboard, plastic, and wood (1/4-in.–1/2-in. plywood); scissors and sturdy tape for hanging the strips on the dowel or wire; a small electric fan

Activity

Children use strips of material of various weights to construct an anemometer, an instrument for measuring the force of the wind. They create "scales" of wind strengths by relating the movement of the strips to the distance from the wind source. They also create a descriptive scale of wind strengths by relating the movement of the graduated strips to other light and strong wind effects, such as flags flying, leaves fluttering, trees bending, water rippling, and so on.

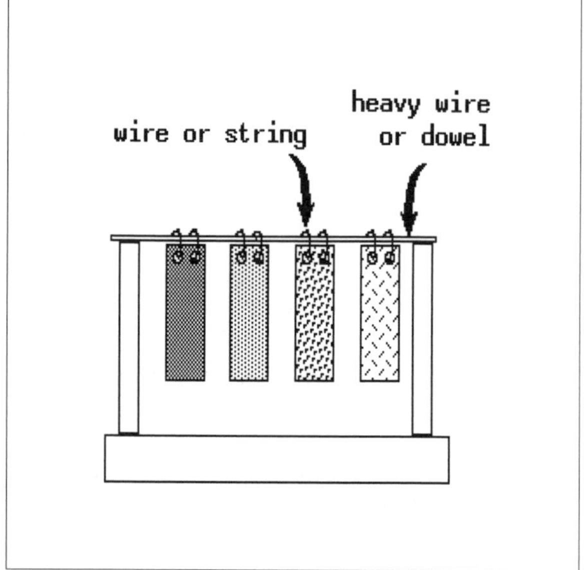

Children have seen a light wind easily move things like leaves, scraps of paper, and dandelion seeds. They know that an even stronger wind enables them to fly a kite or a flag. And a very strong wind can blow over heavy objects—like garbage cans, or bicycles. The anemometer, by using same-sized strips of graduated weight, provides a simple way to judge relative wind strength.

To create a wind scale with their anemometer, children might use the fan to create wind and set it at varying distances from the anemometer, recording the distance from which the wind moves each type of strip. To create a descriptive or observational scale of wind strength (one that can be used without instruments), children might also take the anemometer outside on days with different wind strengths and relate the movement of the various strips to movement of other objects like leaves, flags, and large branches, giving their own descriptive names to the different wind strengths.

Questions to Ask

How can you tell, without feeling it, whether the wind force is strong or weak? What objects are moved by a light wind? What objects are moved by a strong wind? What besides the weight of an object affects the wind's force on the object? How would you describe a wind that moves only the paper strip? Only the paper and cardboard strip? Only the paper, cardboard, and plastic strips? All of the strips?

Extension

1. Children take their anemometer outdoors each day for a week or a month, at the same time each day, and make a graph of wind strengths for the entire period of time.

2. Given a set of materials of varying weights, children order them according to the wind strength that would be required to move each of them

3. Children learn about the Beaufort Scale—about its origins and Admiral Beaufort's life.

Related Reading

Bendick, Jeanne. *The Wind.* Chicago: Rand McNally & Co., 1964.

Catherall, Ed. *Windpower.* Hove, East Sussex, England: Wayland Publishers Limited, 1981.

Watson, Jane Werner. *Alternate Energy Sources.* New York: Franklin Watts, Inc., 1979.

Note: For information on the Beaufort Scale, see any encyclopedia.

Grades 2–3

Making Parachutes

Discovering the effect of moving air on the descent of a parachute

Key Experiences

- Repeating an activity that produces a change to gain awareness of possible causes
- Comparing the performance of similar structures or materials
- Identifying more than one factor affecting the operation or effectiveness of a structure

Materials

For each pair of children: various-sized squares of thin plastic (cut from trash bags, for example), lightweight string or heavy thread, scissors, small weights (e.g., nails, washers, coins), tape, a fan for producing an air stream

Activity

Children construct parachutes of varying sizes and with various amounts of weight attached. They experiment with tossing the various parachutes, all wadded up, into the air and then letting them float to the ground. They also try tossing a wadded-up parachute that is tied so that it cannot unfurl, to see how it falls to the ground. They also direct a fan at the parachute, letting it capture some of the moving air, to see the effect the force of moving air has on a parachute.

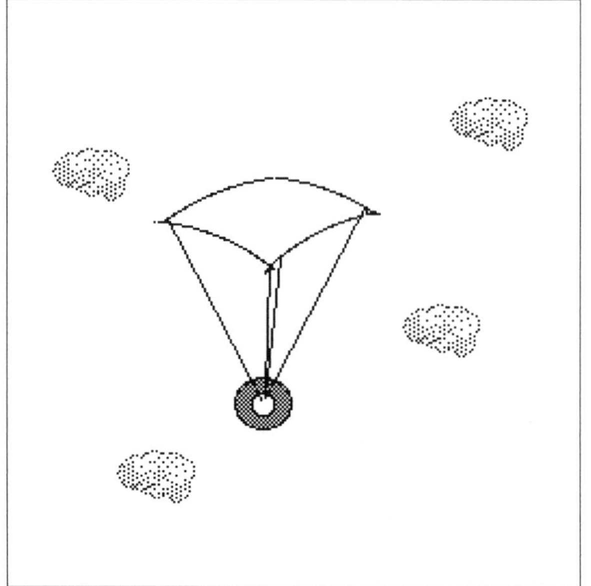

With the parachute, as with any falling object, the force of gravity causes it to fall, but the force of air against the moving parachute retards the fall. When the parachute is open (as opposed to wadded up), it offers a greater area for air resistance, causing it to descend gently, rather than plummet. Though children of this age may not be able to supply such an explanation, they can get some idea that air "pushes" upward on the parachute at the same time that the weights pull it downward. Seeing the effect that the air stream from the fan has on the parachute should help them identify moving air as the source of the upward push.

Questions to Ask

What are the parts of your parachute? What happens when the parachute is tossed up but can't open? What happens when it can open? When is a parachute useful? How does it work? What is the purpose of each of the parts of the parachute? If you changed any of the parts, what effects did that have on your parachute?

Extension

1. Children cut a hole in the middle of the parachute and see how this affects the behavior of the falling chute. They also try making larger and larger holes and observe the effects of these changes.

2. Children use a small spring scale to measure the force on the parachute that is produced by the air stream from a fan. They try this with parachutes of different sizes to compare the fan's effect in each case.

3. Children make a graph showing how long chutes of different sizes take to fall from the same height. They also graph fall times for the same parachute when it has different weights attached.

Related Reading

Adler, Irving and Adler, Ruth. *Air.* New York: The John Day Company, 1962.

Engle, Eloise. *Parachutes, How They Work.* New York: G. P. Putnam's Sons, 1972.

Freeman, Mae. *When Air Moves.* New York: McGraw-Hill Book Co., Inc., 1968.

Grades 2–3

Motion Produced by Sound Energy

Discovering that sound energy creates forces that can make objects move

Key Experiences

- Identifying a cause for a change
- Relating the magnitude of an effect to the magnitude of a cause

Materials

For each pair of children: a large cardboard, plastic, or metal tube 3 in.–4 in. in diameter (e.g., an oatmeal box, a shortening, or coffee can, with both ends removed); thin plastic wrap or rubber from a balloon; a small amount of sand or table salt; and several large rubber bands

Activity

(Suitable for a large group)

Children construct a drum-like sound detector by fastening tightly stretched plastic wrap or a torn balloon over an open end of a tube. They place a few grains of sand on the drumhead and observe the effects when various sounds (such as a clap or musical notes) are produced near the open end of the sound detector. (Placing the detector over the speaker of a radio or tape recorder and playing music or speech at moderate volume will keep the sand or salt grains in motion.)

When the air is set vibrating by the sound energy, this sets the plastic or rubber in motion, making the sand grains bounce on the drumhead. Once they observe this effect, children can experiment with a wide range of sounds and varying distances between the detector and the sound source.

Questions to Ask

What kinds of sounds did you test with your sound detector? What differences did you see in their effects? What happens as the sound source gets farther away from the detector? As it gets closer to the detector? Why do you think sound makes the sand move?

Extension

1. Children "feel" the effects of sound energy by using their sound detector in this way: One child holds the detector and touches his/her fingertips very lightly to the drumhead while another child claps or speaks loudly into the open end of the detector. They also play a musical instrument near the open end and see how the sounds "feel."

2. Children glue a piece of shiny metal foil (½-in. square) to the center of the detector's drumhead. Then they let a light beam shine on the square (in a darkened room) so it reflects onto the wall. When they make various noises into the open end of the detector, they observe the effect on the spot of reflected light. They try various musical notes and see if the effect is the same for each note.

Related Reading

Brandt, Keith. *Sound.* Mahwah, NJ: Troll Associates, 1985.

Kettelkamp, Larry. *The Magic of Sound.* New York: William Morrow & Co., 1982.

Macaulay, David. *The Way Things Work.* Boston: Houghton Mifflin Co., 1988.

Webb, Angela. *Sound.* New York: Franklin Watts, 1988.

Wyler, Rose. *Science Fun With Drums, Bells, & Whistles.* Morristown, NJ: Messner, 1987.

Grades K–3

Making Telephones

Discovering that solid materials can help transfer sound energy over long distances

Materials

For each pair of children: plastic tubing, or garden hose (25 ft–50 ft); two funnels to fit into the ends of the hose or tubing; two large plastic cups (each with a hole punched in the bottom); heavy string (25 ft–50 ft); two washers or buttons; strong tape

Activity

Children construct "string-and-cup" telephones and "tube-and-funnel" telephones. For the string-and-cup phone, they use buttons or washers to tie off the ends of the string after threading it through the cup bottoms, so the string will not pull out. For the tube-and-funnel phone, if necessary, they secure the funnels to the hose (or tube) ends with tape. After making the phones, by taking turns whispering into one end, children can explore the ways sound carries in a tube or across a string. They can test their phones across various distances within the room and also in places where whispers are unlikely to carry, such as from room to room, from inside a partly-closed closet, or around a corner.

Sound energy is a vibration most often carried through the air from source to ear. The hose channels vibrating air from the speaker to listener, helping it to travel longer distances without being blocked by walls and other objects. In the string-and-cup phone, vibration is transferred from air to cup bottom, from cup bottom to string, along the string, from the string to the other cup bottom, and from the cup bottom to air at the other end. Solids (like string) are often better at transferring vibrations than are fluids (like air or water). In fluids, a sound may go off in all directions,

Key Experiences

- Recognizing that a sequence of change involves a sequence of causes and effects
- Comparing the performance of similar structures or materials
- Observing and describing a pattern of change

while in the hose or string, it is confined and thus is preserved over longer distances.

Questions to Ask

What are some places your phones carried your partners' whispers? Could you hear someone whisper from those places without a phone? How far away from your partner can you get and still hear a whisper without a phone? With a phone? Which carries sound better, the string-and-cup phone or the tube-and-funnel phone? Do you think you could use a string (or a tube) for a phone without the cups (funnels)? Could you use two cups (funnels) without the string (tube)? What purpose do the cups (funnels) serve? What does the string (tube) do?

Extension

1. Children substitute different materials for the string—thin wire, nylon fishing line, and see what impact this has on the phone's effectiveness.

2. Children explore other ways sound travels through solid objects and compare this to how it travels through air. For example, they listen to a ticking watch by putting an ear to a table on which the watch is placed, or by putting the watch at one end of a meter stick while holding an ear to the other end. Another exploration is tying some metal objects (e.g., spoons) to one end of a string and holding the other end of the string to one ear while rattling the objects together.

3. Children explore making a "musical instrument" of bottles (or glasses) each filled with a different amount of water. When they tap the bottles lightly they hear the sounds produced by the various amounts of water and often witness the vibration or ripples on the surface of the water.

4. Children explore the sounds they produce with a "musical instrument" made by stretching rubber bands of varying lengths over an open box (a plastic box works nicely). When the bands are plucked, the vibrating band (which can be observed) sets the air next to it vibrating, which sets more air vibrating until it reaches the ear to produce a musical note.

5. Children read about the invention of the telephone and other technological advances of the same era and discuss their impact on people's everyday lives.

Related Reading

Broekel, Ray. *Sound Experiments.* Chicago: Children's Press, 1983.

Kettelkamp, Larry. *The Magic of Sound.* New York: William Morrow & Co., 1982.

Macaulay, David. *The Way Things Work.* Boston: Houghton Mifflin Co., 1988.

Neal, Charles D. *Sound.* Chicago: Follett Publishing Co., 1962.

Grades 2–3

Motion Produced by Heat

Discovering that heat energy can make objects move

Key Experiences

- Identifying a cause for a change
- Recognizing that a sequence of change involves a sequence of causes and effects

Materials

Aluminum or steel bar approximately 1/8 in. × 1 in. × 24 in. (stored in freezer), straight pin, small wood blocks, hair dryer, paper indicator scale made from ordinary typing paper, freezer, tape, electric blow dryer

Activity

(Suitable for a large group)

Children observe the effects of heat on a metal bar, using an apparatus set up by the adult as shown. The adult retrieves the cold bar from the freezer and quickly places it on the pin. The adult or a child warms the bar with the hair dryer and the group observes the turning of the indicator.

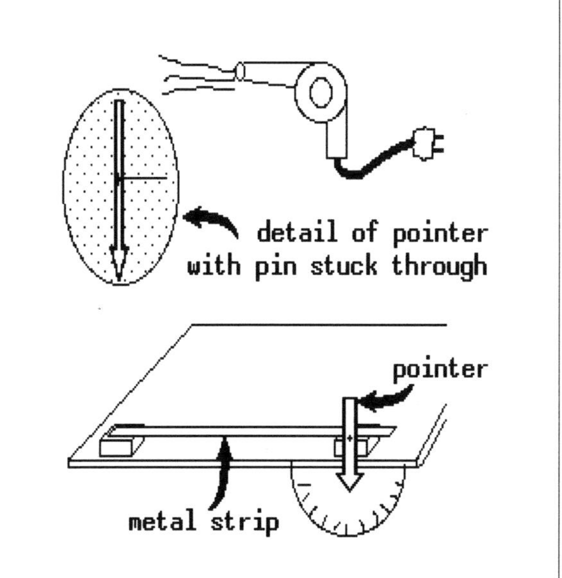

Heat is a form of energy that can make things change. Like wind energy, it can even make objects move. The bar begins to get as warm as the room as it is removed from the freezer, and heat from the blow dryer makes it warmer. As the bar warms, it gets longer, causing the pin to roll and the indicator to move. The change is small, but easily observed. In this activity, heat energy is "made visible," showing its effect by changing the length of the metal bar.

Questions to Ask

What happens when the metal bar is heated? Cooled? How does the heating or cooling make the pointer move? How could we use this same idea to make a thermometer?

Extension

Give each pair of children two identical jars with metal lids. Have the children tighten one of the lids, counting the number of turns. Then repeat with the other jar. Have children heat one of the lids with a hair dryer. They should then try unscrewing both lids, comparing how easily they turn. Have children repeat this test several times and then try to relate this experience to what happened in the previous activity. Have children do the same test with a pair of plastic jars with plastic lids (e.g., a peanut butter jar).

Related Reading

Jennings, Terry. *Heat.* Chicago: Children's Press, 1989.

Oleksy, Walter. *Experiments With Heat.* Chicago: Children's Press, 1986.

Santrey, Lawrence. *Heat.* Mahwah, NJ: Troll Associates, 1985.

Grades 2–3

Building a Water Wheel

Discovering that the force of moving water creates change and transfers energy

Materials

For each child: a thread spool, a knitting needle, a large cork, six or eight rectangular pieces of thin plastic for blades (e.g., milk-jug plastic), a knife (to cut slots in the cork for the blades)

Key Experiences

- Building structures with moving parts
- Identifying a cause for a change

Activity

Children make a water wheel in the following way: After pushing the knitting needle through the cork's center, they make a paddle wheel by inserting the plastic blades in slots in the cork (they may need adult assistance in cutting the slots). Then they slip a spool on the other end of the knitting needle and, using this spool as a handle, hold the paddle wheel under a stream of running water. The force of the water works on the blades (vanes) of the water wheel, changing them from stationary to moving, and transferring energy from water to wheel.

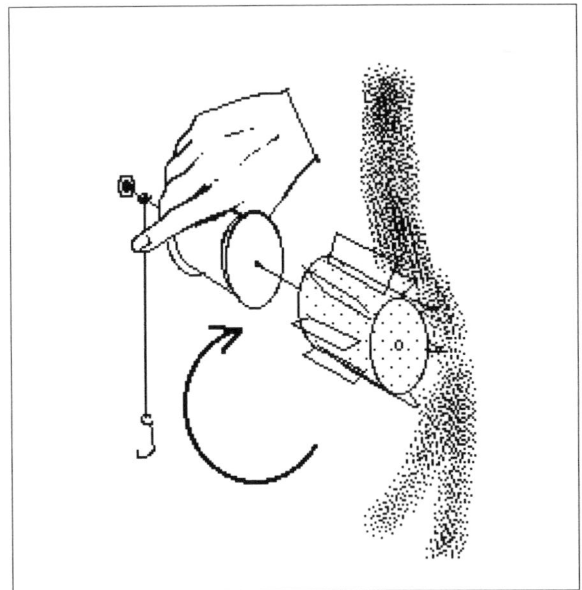

Using a knitting needle thin enough to easily pass through the spool should assure smooth rotation of the paddle wheel. Also, the blades, or vanes, should be spaced out as evenly as possible around the cork.

Questions to Ask

What are the moving parts of the water wheel? What parts do not move? What changes when the water is turned on? What causes this change? Can you think of how a rotating water wheel could produce other changes?

Extension

Children tape a thread or light string to the shaft of the water wheel (the knitting needle) and see how it winds itself around the shaft when the wheel turns. A paper clip "hook" on one end of this string enables the rotating water wheel to lift small objects.

Related Reading

Bailey, Donna. *Energy From Wind & Water.* Austin, TX: Steck-Vaughan, 1990.

Catherall, Ed. *Working With Water* (pp. 24–25, 47). Chicago: Albert Whitman & Co., 1964.

Ford, Betsy. *Water Wheel.* San Francisco, CA: Norton Coker Press, 1990.

Smith, Norman. *Energy Isn't Easy* (pp. 35, 57, 72–73). New York: McCann, Inc., New York, 1984.

Watson, Jane Werner. *Alternate Energy Sources* (pp. 42–43). New York: Franklin Watts, Inc., 1979.

▼

Appendix A

Science Key Experience Checklist

This checklist is designed for recording observations about individual children's progress through the science key experiences. Note that some children may encounter these experiences in a sequence different from the one given here. Also, for some children, progress through one group of key experiences may be more rapid than progress through another group. The developmental levels given are intended to provide only an *approximate* yardstick of progress.

Observing: looking with a purpose; collecting data

Level 1—Preoperations: Intuitive Thinking

☐ Uses all the senses to investigate, explore, and observe the world

☐ Collects materials of many kinds

☐ Observes color, shape, form, or pattern (*circle* color, shape, form *or* pattern *as applicable)*

☐ Initiates an observation to solve a problem or answer a question ("Let's watch and see if that ant makes it across the sidewalk without dropping that big crumb it's carrying.")

Level 2—Early Concrete Operations

☐ Looks at something familiar in a new way: observes closely, systematically, and objectively

☐ Takes something apart to observe it more closely (unravels a piece of yarn to see how the fibers are twisted)

☐ Observes changes over time

☐ Observes the quantity of a material or the frequency of an event

☐ Uses instruments (magnifiers, binoculars, slow-motion camera, tape recorder) to assist observations (*circle applicable instrument)*

Level 3—Late Concrete Operations

☐ Uses audiovisual media for planned and systematic observations (photographing the same tree once a week for a year)

☐ Observes an object from different perspectives

☐ Observes the subsystems of an environment or structure to see how they interact ("We've noticed that the fish die if we don't add enough food, but too much makes the fish tank dirty.")

Classifying and ordering materials according to their attributes and properties

Level 1—Preoperations: Intuitive Thinking

☐ Observes the attributes of objects

☐ Observes similarities and differences ("Both butterflies are spotted,") including differences on a single dimension (bluer, sweeter)

☐ Classifies materials into small groups based on common attributes

Level 2—Early Concrete Operations

☐ Observes multiple similarities and differences ("All the birds in this cage have feathers, wings, and pointed beaks but are many different colors.")

☐ Orders objects according to variation along a single dimension (less rough, smooth, smoother)

☐ Observes similarities and differences in structural patterns and groups objects accordingly ("This group of shells are shaped like fans.")

☐ Classifies materials into two groups based on the presence or absence of one attribute (dissolves in water/doesn't dissolve in water)

Level 3—Late Concrete Operations

☐ Observes symmetry and asymmetry in natural and manufactured objects

☐ Uses an identification guide to look up organisms or nonliving materials (uses books to identify trees or wildflowers)

☐ Classifies or orders using two-dimensional matrices (orders screws by length and diameter)

☐ Classifies hierarchically: groups into categories and subcategories (birds, birds of prey, birds of prey that live in Michigan)

Measuring, testing, and analyzing: assessing the properties and composition of materials

Level 1—Preoperations: Intuitive Thinking

☐ Compares the properties of materials ("This paper folds more easily.")

☐ Measures by producing a length to match another length (cuts a string as long as his/her foot)

☐ Counts events over time ("How many leaves will fall off this tree tonight?")

Level 2—Early Concrete Operations

☐ Measures properties and changes using standard or nonstandard whole units (weighs using the whole units on a scale; measures elapsed time in sand timer cycles)

☐ Uses testing assesses properties by comparing effects of standardized procedures (tests the strength of several fibers by tying them to a standard weight and observing which ones break)

☐ Analyzes: separates and measures the parts of a mixture or material to describe its composition (separates and measures the wheat flakes and raisins in a box of cereal)

☐ Uses standard measuring tools (ruler, thermometer, calipers, scales, timers) (*circle applicable tool*)

☐ Compares the effects produced by increasing or decreasing a causal factor (compares the effect on the color of water of adding a larger quantity of food coloring)

Level 3—Late Concrete Operations

☐ Measures using both whole units and fractions of a unit

☐ Estimates measurements ("It looks like it's about 2 feet tall.")

☐ Uses a scale model to study the features of a larger or smaller object (model of a bicycle gear made from spools and rubber bands)

☐ Measures the increase or decrease in a causal factor in order to relate it to the change in an effect ("Let's see how much farther the car goes if we raise the height of the track 3 in.")

Observing, predicting, and controlling change: understanding causality

Level 1—Preoperations: Intuitive Thinking

- ☐ Observes and identifies a change ("The flower has closed up.")
- ☐ Manipulates physical objects to produce an effect or change (blows out a candle)
- ☐ Repeats an activity that produces a change to gain awareness of possible causes (repeatedly pushes an empty bottle under water and watches as bubbles are released)
- ☐ Identifies a cause for a change ("The leaves are flying through the air. The wind must be blowing.")

Level 2—Early Concrete Operations

- ☐ Observes and describes a pattern of change in events and movements (life cycles, cycles of motion, weather changes)
- ☐ Predicts a change in a situation from observation of change in other similar situations ("The sky is gray and the wind is blowing. I think it's going to rain.")
- ☐ Identifies more than one possible cause for a change ("The lawn mower won't start. Maybe it's out of gas or needs a tune-up. We have the most trouble on chilly days.")
- ☐ Tests an explanation for a change by acting to reverse it ("The plant is wilting; let's try watering it and see if that helps.")

Level 3—Late Concrete Operations

- ☐ Recognizes that a sequence of change (winding up a toy car to make it go) involves a sequence of causes and effects (Winding the key on the car activates motion in a series of gears, eventually resulting in the motion of the car.)
- ☐ Relates the magnitude of an effect to the magnitude of a cause ("A strong wind will cause many more leaves to fall off the tree than a gentle wind.")
- ☐ Begins to recognize that explaining a change may require keeping some variables (possible causes) constant ("I think this toy car goes faster than the other one because it's built differently, but it might be because I oiled it before the race. Let's oil the other car, too, and then try racing them again.")

Designing, building, fabricating, and modifying structures or materials

Level 1—Preoperations: Intuitive Thinking

- ☐ Designs and builds simple structures (makes a garage for toy cars out of blocks and boards)
- ☐ Changes a structure to solve a problem in its design ("Maybe the tower won't fall over if I use the flat blocks instead.")
- ☐ Compares the performance of similar structures or materials ("The ramp works better this way.")
- ☐ Uses plans supplied by others to make a simple structure or material (a paper teepee; flour paste)

Level 2—Early Concrete Operations

- ☐ Designs and builds more complex structures (realistic objects constructed with conventional building materials, tools, and fasteners)
- ☐ Builds simple containers or environments for living things (an insect box; a windowbox garden)
- ☐ Improves a structure or material through trial-and-error modifications (varying the height and length of a ramp to increase the speed of a toy car; adding sugar or water to icing to change the consistency)
- ☐ Uses plans supplied by others to make a more complex and functional structure or material (making dog biscuits, making pinwheels)

Level 3—Late Concrete Operations

- ☐ Builds structures with moving parts (latches, hinges, wheels, and axles)
- ☐ Builds with simple electrical circuits
- ☐ Analyzes and solves problems in a structure by taking it apart, modifying parts, and rebuilding it (troubleshoots a problem in a wind-up car by separately examining the wheels and axles, the spring mechanism, and the gears)
- ☐ Identifies more than one factor affecting the operation or effectiveness of a structure or material (recognizing that the problem of fastening two materials together may be affected by the type of fastener—e.g., tape, screws, nails—the size of the fastener, the smoothness of the surfaces being joined, and the weight of the pieces to be joined)

Reporting and interpreting data and results

Level 1—Preoperations: Intuitive Thinking

- ☐ Discusses observations
- ☐ Begins to use scientific terms and comparative vocabulary in reporting observations
- ☐ Reports sequences of events
- ☐ Reports and represents observations using drawings, tape recordings, photos, or real objects mounted on charts

Level 2—Early Concrete Operations

- ☐ Records and displays numerical data
- ☐ Uses models, drawings, and diagrams to illustrate oral or written reports
- ☐ Arranges collections and displays to present findings
- ☐ Uses books, pictures, charts, and computers to gain further information

Level 3—Late Concrete Operations

- ☐ Defines technical terms in science reporting
- ☐ Uses bar graphs, line graphs, and tables to present data
- ☐ Makes models of objects and systems to show how they work (making a model of a stream bed, using sand and buckets of water)

▼

Appendix B

Materials for Science

Below we set out suggestions for materials and equipment under the main themes of the science curriculum. Note that some items are repeated in several lists, under different headings. This was done deliberately, to make it easier for teachers to gather materials for specific kinds of activities.

Life and Environment Materials

The materials needed for life and environment activities include a variety of containers and tools for collecting and displaying living things, common living materials for testing and analyzing, containers for housing animals, food to keep them alive, and so forth. Very little specialized equipment must be purchased for activities under this general theme.

Containers for gathering and storing collections

- Plastic bags of all sizes, including strong ones for heavy loads (soils, rocks, wood samples); small pocket-sized bags; zip-type bags for spillable samples, seeds, sand, small leaves
- Plastic boxes of all kinds, especially transparent ones with screw-tops or stoppers
- Paintbrushes, spoons, and paper tubes for picking up small animals without hurting them
- Small- and medium-sized plastic buckets (not too large), some with lids, for carrying liquids
- See-through plastic containers of all kinds (not glass)
- Plastic water jugs with tops cut off (for use as storage containers); cut-off tops of plastic jugs (for use as funnels)

- White enamel plates or pie dishes for observing small animals, especially water creatures
- Cardboard boxes of all sizes, preferably those that stack inside each other

Tools for collecting

- Small spade (not large enough to damage the natural environment)
- Two or three small trowels
- Several large spoons
- Several pairs of scissors
- Household sieve or strainer
- Blunt table knives (for digging and scraping)
- Pruning shears (for teacher's use)
- String (for measuring), tape measures, rulers
- Tweezers

Food for animals in insect cages and terraria

- Ants—bread crumbs, small food scraps, sugar-water solution, crumbled peanuts, honey, molasses, water (to be placed on the top of the soil where the ants live, or in a small shallow container nearby)
- Butterflies—fresh, thick sugar-water or honey-water solution, flowers (from which they can take nectar)
- Caterpillars—the leaves of plants the animals were found on (supplied fresh daily)
- Crickets—pulpy fruits, lettuce, bread crumbs, peanut butter, crushed seeds
- Grasshoppers—the leaves they were eating when found, celery, ripe bananas
- Common moth larvae and their preferred leaves: Cecropia (willow, maple, apple); Polyphemus (willow, oak, apple, plum birch); Promethia (wild cherry, ash, lilac, tulip tree); Luna (hickory, walnut, sweet gum); Cynthia (lilac, sycamore, cherry)
- Snails (land)—lettuce, celery tops, spinach, grapes, apple pieces
- Snails (water)—fish food, lettuce, aquarium plants, spinach, dried shrimp

- Tadpoles (vegetarian stage)—water plants or green algae scum in tank; cooked oatmeal, cooked spinach, lettuce
- Tadpoles (meat-eating stage)—small pieces of hamburger in very small quantities
- Wild birds at feeders—wild bird seed (store-bought), small seeds from wild flowers, peanut butter, bread in very small pieces, suet, raisins, apple pieces, sunflower seeds, unsalted nuts, bird pudding, water

Desirable (but not essential) specialized equipment

- Inexpensive stopwatch (for measuring animal movement in seconds)
- Binoculars (not high-powered, x 6 or x 8)
- Spring balances, one for very light weights, one for medium loads up to 5-lb
- Large, low-power magnifying glasses (4-in. diameter)
- Aquarium tank

Common kitchen supplies

- Bread
- Breakfast cereals
- Corn flour
- Salt
- Jam
- Olive oil
- Bouillon cubes
- Butter
- Cheese
- Honey
- Vinegar
- Milk
- Plain flour
- Maple syrup
- Coconut (dried and fresh)
- Lard
- Meat drippings
- Sugar
- Jello
- Suet

Fruits and vegetables useful for experiments

- Apples
- Bananas
- Dried foods:
- Raisins
- Peas
- Beans
- Apricots
- Dates
- Green cabbage
- Red cabbage
- Carrots
- Celery
- Raspberries
- Tomatoes
- Potatoes
- Lemons
- Oranges
- Onions
- Parsnips
- Strawberries

Plant materials useful for experiments

- Geraniums and easy-to-grow potted plants, the greater the variety the better
- Seeds: bean, cress, corn, grass, mustard, pea, radish, sunflower, sweet pea
- Flowers: buttercup, sweet pea, nasturtium, daisy
- Other fruits and seeds: acorns, horse chestnuts, rose hips, sycamore
- All plants of the cabbage family (for excellent large-scale examples of plant forms)

Structure and Form Materials

The materials useful for structure and form activities include a variety of readily available everyday materials and a few purchased tools and instruments. Testing and analyzing of properties is one major category of activity that can usually be carried out with materials available in any household or those easily collected outdoors by children.

Man-made structures provide another source of activities. The structures that can be observed in the environment—bridges, buildings under construction, etc.—provide one type of material that can be a springboard for activities focusing on shapes, methods of construction, or strengths of various structures. Students can also be encouraged to build their own structures with wood scraps, cardboard, and other simple materials.

General materials—collected, easily obtained, purchased

Collected materials

- Plastic bottles, containers
- Rubber and plastic suction cups
- Rubber plungers
- Cans
- Wooden boxes
- Cardboard boxes, with and without lids
- Corks
- Bottlecaps
- Cardboard tubes
- Spools
- Corrugated cardboard
- Newspaper
- Wire
- Nuts and bolts
- Nails
- Small and large plastic bags
- House bricks
- Wooden blocks, wood scraps
- String
- Cloth samples, all kinds
- Short lengths of cord and rope
- Knitting yarn
- Cotton and nylon threads
- Plastic foam pieces
- Wood shavings
- Sawdust
- Sand

Easily obtained materials

- Glue or strong paste
- Stiff strips of cardboard (for framing structures)
- Paper fasteners
- Scissors
- Staplers
- Rulers
- Bulldog clips
- Rubber bands
- Strips of pegboard
- Drinking straws
- Lengths of cane, dowels
- Thin sticks (for supporting plants)
- Cellophane tape, various widths
- Blotting paper
- Metal foil
- Wax paper
- Balsa wood (strips, sheets, blocks)
- Balsa cement
- Broom handles
- Balls (rubber, foam, inflated)

Purchased materials

- Spring balances, both metric and English, at least one of each to measure the following ranges: 0–½ lb, 0–7 lb, 0–28 lb, 0–100 g, 0–5 kg, 0–20 kg
- Kitchen scale and weights
- Range of nails to use as weights, ½-in–2-in.
- Stopwatch
- Hammer
- Needlenose pliers
- Wire-cutting pliers
- Screwdrivers (small and medium)
- Junior hack saw
- Small vice
- File

Materials for specific topics

Rock study

- Locally found rocks
- Igneous rocks: granite, quartz, pumice, basalt

- Sedimentary rocks: sandstone, clay, limestone, conglomerate, coal
- Artificial stones: various house bricks, concrete in various forms, tiles, roofing, floor tiles, wall tiles, plaster of Paris objects

Fiber study

- Paper and cardboard (all kinds)
- String, rope (all kinds)
- Sackcloth, wood shavings
- Cloths (samples): wool, cotton, silk, synthetics, natural/synthetic blends

Buoyancy study

- Equal-sized wooden blocks (balsa, oak, pine, etc.)
- Cork
- Plastic foam
- Sponges
- Pumice
- Clay
- Plastic tubing
- Plastic bottles

Water-solubility study

- Salt
- Sugar
- Washing soda
- Chalk
- Talcum powder
- Baking powder
- Soap powder
- Coffee
- Tea
- Scouring powder
- Sand

Absorbency study

- Paper towels
- Fabric samples: cotton, silk, wool, etc.
- Food coloring
- Building materials: wood, concrete, bricks, etc.
- Sugar lumps

Energy and Change Materials

The theme of energy and change offers a wide range of possible activities, many of which involve children directly in manipulating everyday materials. Because these kinds of activities call for more apparatus, whether child-created or teacher-supplied, lists of materials are presented for several major topics within this theme. We have listed only a few materials for studying chemical change, because many of the suitable materials either have already been listed under other topics or will be collected by the children themselves in the course of science activities.

Materials for studying machines

Collected materials

- Wheels of all kinds and items to serve as wheels—spools, thread reels, circular lids
- Nails of various lengths including some long ones to serve as axles and spindles
- Wood pieces, all lengths, and shapes
- Cardboard boxes, all sizes and shapes
- Wooden blocks (for supporting apparatus)
- Wire of various kinds and stiffness
- House bricks
- Buttons and small beads (for use as washers)
- Hairpins
- Paper clips
- Plastic containers, all sizes
- String, rope, and cord
- Saucers
- Sand and sawdust
- Knitting needles, especially easy-to-cut plastic one

Easily obtained materials

- Stiff strips of cardboard (for framing structures)
- Brass paper fasteners, large-size
- Sandpaper of various grades
- Small screw hooks and screw eyes
- Plastic tubing
- Broom handles
- Tape measures, rulers, yardstick, meter stick (30 cm to 1 m)
- Rubber bands and elastic strips

- Glass marbles
- Pulleys
- Wood cubes of various sizes and woods
- Bowls
- Buckets
- Glue
- Cellophane tape
- Springs, various kinds

Purchased materials

- Spring balances, at least one of each, to measure the following ranges: 0–½ lb, 0–7 lb, 0–28 lb, 0–100 g, 0–5 kg, 0–20 kg
- Sets of weights in the following ranges: 1 oz–1 lb, 25–250 g
- Stop watch
- Hammer
- Wire cutters
- Pliers

Materials for studying heat, light, and sound

Collected materials

- Pieces of wood and wooden blocks for bases and holders
- Transparent and translucent materials (preferably plastic, not glass)
- Cardboard boxes and tubes
- Handbag mirrors of all sizes with backs covered with stick-on labels or adhesive shelf paper for safety
- Shiny spoons, all sizes (to use as reflectors)
- Cut glass bottle stoppers (for refraction)
- Materials in bright colors
- Fabric of all sorts
- Tin cans
- Clay plant pots, many sizes
- Long nails
- Pieces of metal rod
- Metal strips with the ends filed smooth
- Plastic containers with lids or stoppers
- Plastic tubing
- Rubber balloons of different sizes

- Combs
- Metal cups or mugs
- Black, white, and colored paper
- Plastic foam pieces

Easily obtained materials

- Tracing paper
- Curved shaving mirror
- Musical toys
- Wind-up watch or clock
- Small bells
- Guitar strings
- Black paint
- Cotton batting, blanket scraps, and other sound-absorbing materials
- Corks
- Aluminum paint
- Collection of similar objects (e.g., spoons of similar sizes) made of different materials: plastic, wood, iron, brass

Purchased materials

- Magnifying glasses
- 60° prisms (inexpensive, molded, not optically worked)
- Hand lenses, 4-in. diameter
- Tuning forks (one or two of different pitches)
- Thermometers (wall type)
- One "unbreakable" bath thermometer

Materials for studying magnetism and electricity

Collected materials

- Magnets (horseshoe, bar, circular, magnetic strip)
- Toy magnetic compasses
- Pieces of steel strip, e.g., old hacksaw blades
- Steel knitting needles
- Bodkin or crewel needles
- Materials for testing with magnets (metal, plastic, or wood items or items with metal cores covered with paint, plastic, or fabric)
- Corks
- Bottlecaps
- Plastic bottles

- Metal strips
- Bulldog clips
- Nails up to to 6-in.,
- Screws up to ½-in.
- Metal foil
- Scrap wire
- Strong thread or very thin string
- Rubber bands
- Thumbtacks
- Plastic, metal paper clips

Easily obtained materials

- Cellophane tape
- Cotton thread
- Glue or paste
- Pencils
- Rulers
- Screw eyes
- Small screw hooks
- Plastic containers (for floating)
- Magnetic toys
- Hardboard or wooden pieces (for use as bases for apparatus)
- Scissors
- Materials for testing conductivity: various metals, wood, plastic, etc.

Purchased materials

- Strong bar magnets, at least 4
- Bell wire, #22
- Covered wire, #24
- Miniature bulb holders with bulbs to fit (in voltages to suit available batteries)
- Electric bell, 3.5- or 4.5-volt
- Screwdrivers, small and medium
- Hammer
- Wire-cutting pliers
- Wire stripper
- Needlenose pliers
- Bradawl
- Batteries for bulbs and bell

Materials for exploring hot air and moving air

- Paper (tissue, crepe)
- Cooking foil
- Radiator
- Steel knitting needle

Kitchen supplies for studying chemical changes

- Baking powder
- Bicarbonate of soda
- Jello
- Sugars (lump, granulated, brown, caster, rock)
- Salt
- Pepper
- Vinegar
- Flour
- Epsom salts
- Health salts
- Cooking oil
- Scouring powder
- Detergent
- Soap
- Soda
- Starch

About the Authors

In his long and multifaceted career, British author and educator **Frank F. Blackwell** has contributed to science education in a wide range of professional roles. Originally a classroom teacher and headmaster at the early childhood, primary, and secondary levels, Blackwell later served as an inspector of schools and a university lecturer in teacher education. He became involved in the development of children's science curricula during the 1960s as a Nuffield Foundation Research Fellow in Science Education, serving on the team that developed the Nuffield Junior Science Project series. In addition, he has authored several other series of science curriculum materials developed by commercial publishers. He has also served on numerous editorial boards and panels overseeing the development of curriculum and reference materials for children, and training publications for teachers. His contributions to science education extend to radio and television, where he has served as a script-writer, consultant, and researcher for science programming. Blackwell has been a consultant to the High/Scope Educational Research Foundation for many years. This volume in the High/Scope K–3 Curriculum Series is his first title for the High/Scope Press.

Frank F. Blackwell

Educational psychologist **Charles Hohmann** has directed the development of the High/Scope Curriculum since 1972. During this time he has been heavily involved in training elementary school teachers as part of the National Follow Through Program for disadvantaged children. Hohmann has a special interest in science education, having obtained an undergraduate degree in physics and having worked in the public schools as a general science teacher. He has developed science learning activities for High/Scope programs serving preschoolers, school-age children, and teens. Hohmann is directing the development and fieldtesting of the entire K–3 Curriculum Series; he is also the author of the *Mathematics* volume in the series. In addition, Hohmann conducts workshops for educators throughout the United States on K–3 education and on computer learning for young children, and he is the author of *Young Children & Computers*, another publication of the High/Scope Press.

Charles Hohmann